This cookbook, my second labor of love, is dedicated to every Low Carber who has ever pondered the question "Who cares about the total carbs - if it doesn't taste good?"

Copyright 2003, Karen M. Rysavy
~ All Rights Reserved ~

ISBN 0-9714929-2-1

Truly Low Carb, Inc.
P.O. Box 1192
Gypsum, Colorado 81637-1192
U.S.A.

INTRODUCTION & RECIPE NOTES 5

APPETIZERS, SNACKS & BEVERAGES

SAUCES, SPREADS & SALAD DRESSINGS

SIDE DISHES, SALADS & VEGETABLES

MAIN DISHES, CASSEROLES & SOUPS

FABULOUS FAKES

Introduction & Recipe Notes

It is with great pleasure that I present this second volume of recipes. Much has happened to me in the three years since my first volume was published, but my low carb eating has remained constant. In fact, it is the rock upon which I draw strength. No matter what else may go other than planned in my life, *this* is something I *can* control. My doctor visits, lab tests, and energy levels continue to encourage me to eat this way forever, and I am happy to do so.

The popularity of low carb eating continues to grow, which means that more pre-made "convenience" items are available all the time. I firmly believe, however, that people do best on this type of plan when they do the majority of their food preparation themselves and stick to the basics as much as possible. I hope my simple-as-possible recipes will help you enjoy doing more of your own food prep.

Sugar alcohols (SA)s can make maintenance a real pleasure, but they can also wreak havoc on some individual's blood sugar and/or weight loss efforts (not to mention the gastric distress they cause others). I therefore specify the use of SAs very rarely - only when necessary for the successful outcome to a particular recipe. You can always substitute maltitol for Splenda™ in my recipes if you so desire, but in those instances when I do specify a SA powder or syrup, please don't attempt to substitute something like Splenda™ in its place. You can usually substitute sugar free honey or maple syrup substitutes made with sorbitol and/or maltitol for maltitol syrup with good results, but you must realize that the taste of your end result may be off.

Nutritional data for all recipes is complete as listed - if you subtract fiber and/or sugar alcohols from your carb counts, then you can and should subtract them from the total carbs listed here. Maltitol syrup was analyzed at 6 SA carbs and 24 calories per Tb. Maltitol powder was calculated at 52.5 SA carbs and

210 calories per 2/3 cup (100 g). These are averages, which are based on my best judgment regarding conflicting product laws, regulations and labels at the time of publication.

Yogurt is counted according to standard labels and carbs have not been adjusted.

When I list variations for an ingredient or a recipe, I always analyze it (and usually prefer to make it) using it the first choice listed.

SF stands for "Sugar Free" (a space consideration).

In recipes that call for protein powder, I am referring to shake mix. I figured carb counts based on using a brand with 6 carbs per cup (average at the time of publication). Please be aware that different brands can yield very different results, and may necessitate adjustments to listed liquid measurements. (In other words, if batter that calls for protein powder looks too thick or too thin to you - it probably is.)

Because product availability and ingredients change so often, specific brand recommendations are listed only on the website, where they can be updated as needed. Feedback in this area is encouraged, via the Message Board, for the benefit of all.

Almond flour, unsweetened coconut, flax seeds, and other low carb staples are often sold in bulk in the U.S., bearing no nutrition label (or worse, incorrect data). Please be advised that my nutritional counts are based on "average" product labels and USDA data, applied to weights and measures tested personally by Yours Truly. There are many ways to artificially lower the carb count of a recipe - but I do not do so! I pride myself on real portions and honest, accurate analysis.

Recipes in this volume that specify bake mix were analyzed based on the version included herein. If you own Volume I and prefer to substitute one of the other mixes, your results should be fine, but your nutritional analysis will vary a little. By the same token, if you make Volume I recipes using the Volume II Bake mix, you will achieve a slightly lower overall carb count.

LEGAL DISCLAIMER: No laboratory analysis has been performed on any of the recipes herein. No guarantee is being made as to the accuracy of nutritional statements and no liability will be assumed for any errors. This book does not attempt to provide complete instructions regarding cooking and safety procedures. None of the recipes or material herein should be used as, or construed to be, medical advice of any kind. No one should ever undertake any weight loss, nutritional, or exercise program of any kind without prior consultation with, and continual monitoring by, a qualified physician.

In other words: I do all my recipe analysis personally *based on the best information available to me at the time*. I find mistakes on manufacturer labels all the time. Since I cannot even guarantee the accuracy of information provided by manufacturers for individual ingredients, whose labels are constantly changing, I certainly can't guarantee that the dish you end up with will *exactly* match the analysis I provide. If you are a serious dieter, it would be best for you to always count your own carbs, calories, etc., based on your own products and current labels.

This book is not intended to serve as a diet plan itself. Doctors like the late Robert C. Atkins, M.D., to whom millions of us owe so much, design sound diets - I just create recipes. Please educate yourself about low carb eating and see a doctor regularly. Have lab tests done both before and during any diet plan so that your improved results can serve as additional motivation to establish better, healthier eating habits for a lifetime.

Black Bean Dip

2 cans black soy beans, 15 oz. each
2 Tb. olive oil
1/2 cup chopped onion
2-3 fresh jalapeno peppers (may substitute canned chili peppers if necessary)
2 tsp. minced garlic
1/2 tsp. ground oregano
1/2 tsp. ground cumin
1/2 tsp. salt
1/2 tsp. cayenne pepper
4 oz. cream cheese, cubed

Mince the onion and the jalapeno peppers. (I prefer to use a food processor, and to remove the stems but not the seeds from the peppers, for extra kick.) Heat oil in a medium saucepan; add onion and peppers and sauté until soft and translucent. Add spices and cook for another minute. Meanwhile, drain and rinse one can of the beans. Puree the other can (do not drain off this juice.) Add whole beans and bean puree to the pan, followed by the cubed cream cheese, and continue to cook and stir the mixture until smooth, heated through, and the proper consistency. Mash the whole beans partly while cooking, if desired.

At this point, I usually transfer this to a slow cooker and serve it a little at a time (great for parties!), but it is good cold as well, or reheated in the microwave. Also excellent over nachos, as a sauce, in casseroles, in wraps paired with tortilla meat, etc. You can dress this up by adding diced tomatoes or salsa, cheddar or other cheeses, etc., but it is very good plain.

Makes 4 cups - per 1/2 cup: 192 cal, 14 g fat (4 g sat.), 8 g carb (6 g fiber), 10 g protein.

Buffalo Nips

2 cups walnuts
2 cups almonds
1 cup macadamia nuts
1 cup All-Bran™ Extra Fiber cereal
4 Tb. butter
2/3 cup hot wing sauce (I like Frank's Redhot™)
1 Tb. HOT pepper sauce (such as Tabasco™)
1 Tb. lime juice (fresh or bottled)
2 tsp. garlic (powder, minced, or roasted)

Preheat oven to 375 F. Combine nuts and cereal; set aside. (Use absolutely any combination of nuts and seeds you desire, but nutritional analysis has been based on this combination.) Melt butter; add wing sauce, hot pepper sauce, lime juice, and garlic; blend well. Toss sauce over nuts and cereal. Spread out in 13x9 or larger pan and bake for 25-40 minutes, as needed until crunchy throughout, stirring every five to ten minutes. Watch carefully towards the end to prevent sudden over browning. *Makes 5 cups - per half-cup: 433 cal, 39 g fat (6 g sat.), 14 g carbohydrate (8 g fiber), 10 g protein*

VARIATIONS: Replace the 1 cup cereal with two cups air-popped popcorn. Because the popcorn shrinks, I count the same yield, 10 half-cup servings, at *417 cal, 39g fat (6 sat), 11 carbs (5 fiber) and 10 g protein, each.* May also omit cereal or popcorn completely and use all nuts - in that case, 10 srv = *410 cal, 38.5 g fat (6 sat), 10 g carb (5 g fiber) and 9 g protein, each.*

Did you know...

Walnuts contain a significant amount of Vitamin E, as well as a host of other important vitamins, minerals, and antioxidants. Among tree nuts, walnuts are distinctive in their high concentration of omega-3 fatty acids.

Cilantro Lime de Gallo

14.5 oz. can diced Mexican style tomatoes, drained
1 cup finely minced celery
1/4 cup minced, fresh cilantro, chopped
1 fresh jalapeno pepper, seeded and minced
1 cup diced bell pepper (mixed colors look best)
1/2 cup finely diced onion (I prefer red)
2 Tb. oil
1 Tb. Splenda™ granular
1 Tb. lime juice (fresh or bottled, add to taste)
1/2 tsp. each: salt and pepper
Simply toss ingredients together. Best after sitting for at least 30 minutes. We use this like a relish and put it over almost anything. We also scoop it like salsa. *Makes 3 cups - per 1/4 cup: 33 cal, 2.3 g fat (0 sat.), 3 g carb*

Cinnamon or Garlic Glazed Nuts

4 Tb. butter
1 tsp. ground cinnamon (or 2 tsp. garlic powder)
1 cup Splenda™ granular (only use 1/4 cup with garlic)
1/2 tsp. salt
4 cups walnuts
<u>CINNAMON</u>: Melt butter in a large nonstick pan, add nuts, and toss and cook over medium heat until nuts are aromatic and toasted. Mix remaining ingredients and toss slightly cooled nuts in the mixture. (Nuts may seem soft until fully cooled but should become crisp after cooling, at which point you can store them in an air-tight container for up to two weeks.
<u>GARLIC</u>: Melt butter and add remaining ingredients in order listed. Splenda may seize up into clumps - just break the clumps into small pieces if so, and proceed cooking the mixture for about five minutes, until lightly browned. *Makes 4 cups - per half cup: 377 cal, 35 g fat (5 g sat.), 9 g carb (2 g fiber), 12 g protein*
VARIATIONS: Use other nuts or spices. I especially enjoy pecans. Add some Worcestershire to savory mixes. Go nuts - these are so fast, easy and delicious you could invent a new mix every week!

Coconut Crunch

4 cups pecans (or walnuts, or any combination)
2 cups walnuts (or unsalted hazelnuts)
2 cups macadamia nuts (unsalted, or almonds)
1-1/2 cups grated, unsweetened coconut
1/2 cup SF syrup (vanilla or any flavor)
1 cup granular Splenda™
2 egg whites

Preheat oven to 350 F. Toss nuts in a large bowl with coconut. Drizzle with sugar free syrup and toss until coconut begins to clump with nuts. Whip egg whites with Splenda until soft peaks form. Gently combine egg whites and nuts; spread out onto lined or greased shallow pan and bake 20-40 minutes, stirring occasionally and breaking up larger pieces, until crisp throughout. (Times can vary greatly depending on local humidity and other factors, so watch carefully and adjust as needed.) *Makes 9 cups - per half cup: 343 cal, 35 g fat (4 g sat.), 8 g carb (3 g fiber), 5 g protein*

VARIATIONS: Substitute other nuts; add dried fruits.

Coffee Liqueur

4 cups granular Splenda™
2 Tb. ThickenThin NotStarch™ or 2 tsp. guar gum
2 tsp. instant coffee granules
4 cups brewed coffee
4 tsp. vanilla extract
2 cups good-quality vodka (optional)

Whisk Splenda, starch, and instant coffee together in a saucepan. Slowly whisk in the hot brewed coffee, and continue to stir over medium heat until it comes to a full rolling boil. Remove from heat. Cool completely before adding vodka and vanilla extract.

With vodka included, may be stored at room temperature a long time, then mixed with cream and served over ice as desired. If made without vodka, must be refrigerated and consumed within 7-10 days. *Makes 6 cups - per 2 fl. oz: 63 cal, 0 g fat, 4 g carb, 0 g protein*

Deluxe Mudslides

6 Tb. instant coffee granules
2 Tb. unsweetened cocoa powder
2 Tb. ThickenThin NotStarch™ or 2 tsp. guar gum
2 cups granular Splenda™
2 cups water
1 cup maltitol syrup
1 Tb. vanilla extract
4 cups half and half cream
1 cup heavy cream
2 cups vodka

Whisk coffee, cocoa, starch and Splenda together in large saucepan. Gradually add water and syrup; cook and stir over medium-high heat until mixture comes to a boil. Continue to boil for about ten minutes, to reduce slightly. Cool completely, then add vanilla, vodka, and cream.

Makes 9 cups - per 1/2 cup: 245 cal, 11 g fat (6 g sat.), 23 g carb (0 g fiber, 17 g SA), 2 g protein

Classic Clam Dip

8 oz. cream cheese, softened
2 tsp. minced garlic
2 tsp. Worcestershire sauce
2 tsp. lemon juice
1 tsp. dried onion flakes
1/2 tsp. each: salt and white pepper
7 oz. canned clams; drained and minced

Blend cream cheese and spices together well; fold in clams and allow to set for two+ hours before serving (overnight is better). May be thinned if needed or as desired, with clam juice, cream, sour cream, or additional lemon juice. *Makes 1 cup - per 2 Tb: 140 cal, 11 g fat (6 g sat.), 2 g carb, 8 g protein*

Excellent with shrimp instead of clams.

Hot Artichoke Dip

8 oz. cream cheese, softened
1/2 cup sour cream
1/2 cup mayonnaise
1 tsp. garlic powder
2 tsp. lemon juice
2 cups canned artichoke hearts, drained and minced
1/2 cup grated Parmesan cheese
Blend ingredients together (except for Parmesan cheese). Bake at 400 F till hot and bubbly, about 25 minutes; top with cheese and bake for an additional 5-10 minutes. *Makes 4 cups - per 4 Tb: 133 cal, 12.6 g fat (5 g sat.), 2 g carb, 2 g protein* Excellent with spinach, crab meat, shrimp, or bacon bits instead of *or in addition to* artichokes.

Toasted Onion Dip

2 cups sour cream
3 Tb. dry onion flakes
1-1/2 Tb. onion powder
1 tsp. granular Splenda™
1/2 tsp. salt
1/2 tsp. garlic powder
Blend ingredients and allow to set for at least two hours before serving. *Makes 2 cups - per 4 Tb: 131 cal, 12 g fat (7 g sat.), 5 g carb, 2 g protein*

Fresh Tuna Poppers

12 fresh jalapeno peppers
6 oz. albacore tuna, well drained (two 3-oz. cans)
2/3 cup mayonnaise
1/2 cup minced celery
1/4 cup minced green onion
2 Tb. dill relish
1 Tb. lemon juice
1 Tb. canned pimento
1/2 tsp. salt
Slice peppers in half, long ways. Carefully remove all interior seeds and membranes. Mix remaining ingredients and use to stuff pepper halves. *Makes 24 - per two: 149 cal, 13 g fat (1 g sat.), 1 g carb, 3 g protein*

Garlic & Onion Macadamias

4 cups whole, unsalted macadamias (24 oz. - or use salted nuts and omit added salt)
4 tsp. onion powder
2 tsp. garlic powder
2 tsp. dried parsley
1/2 tsp. salt

Mix spices and set aside. Place nuts in a shallow pan and roast in a slow 275 F oven until their natural oils begin to come out and coat them and they look "greasy" - about 15-20 minutes. At this point, mix the remaining ingredients and add them to the pan. Shake to coat , and continue to roast and shake pan occasionally until the nuts take on a good aroma and are slightly golden. Discard any spices that don't stick. Cool completely and store tightly covered. RECIPE NOTES: Nuts will not become crisp until cool - do not overcook. If nuts do not produce oil as expected, mist with added oil to enable spices to stick. *Makes 4 cups - per 1/2 cup: 488 cal, 52 g fat (7 g sat), 10 g carb (6 g fiber), 5 g protein*

Grilled Stuffed Peppers

12 fresh jalapeno peppers
6 slices thick bacon
8 oz. cream cheese
2 Tb. grated onion
2 tsp. garlic (roasted, minced, or powdered)
1 tsp. diced pimento

Slice jalapenos lengthways and remove interior seeds and membranes. Beat softened cream cheese with garlic, pimento, onion, and parsley. Cut each slice of bacon in half so you get 12 short pieces. Fill pepper halves with creamed mixture, then place them back together, wrap a piece of bacon tightly around them, and secure the whole package with a wooden toothpick or two. Grill over medium heat, turning as needed, for 15-40 minutes, depending on grill temperature, until the bacon is crisp and the pepper is soft. *Makes 12 - per each: 153 cal, 14 g fat (4 g sat), 1 g carb, 5 g protein*

Kettle Corn

8 cups air or microwave-popped popcorn
3 Tb. butter
3 Tb. granular Splenda™
1/2 tsp. salt

Melt butter; whisk in Splenda and salt. Drizzle mixture slowly over pre-popped corn, while shaking bowl or bag from side to side. *Makes 8 cups - per 2 cups: 143 cal, 9 g fat (5 g sat), 13 g carb (2 g fiber), 2 g protein*

Perfect Margaritas

2 fluid oz. tequila (I prefer a good agave like Anejõ 1800 Reserve™)
1 fluid oz. Grand Marnier™ (orange-flavored liqueur)
1 fluid oz. Triple sec
1 fluid oz. fresh lime juice
4-5 fluid oz. prepared sugar free lemonade

Use a shot glass for easiest measuring. I like to mix these ingredients over ice in a shaker cup and then strain it out into salted martini glasses, serving "up" . You can also add ice and blend this for a frozen margarita, but I usually find that I need to add a little sweetener when I do that. Not *extremely* low in carbs, but far preferable to traditional ones.

2 servings, each: 118 cal, 10 g carb
* Omit Triple Sec: 68 cal, 4 g carb, each

Pina Coladas

2 cups ice cubes
3 fluid oz. light rum
1/3 cup unsweetened coconut milk, canned
1 tsp. natural pineapple flavoring (adjust for differences in taste and strength between brands)
1/3 cup granular Splenda™

Mix ingredients in blender and puree. Taste and adjust as needed for individual tastes.

1 serving: 302 cal, 9 g fat (8 g sat), 6 g carb, 1 g protein

VARIATIONS: Add coconut extract as well, or substitute SF syrups for Splenda and/or extracts.

Sausage Balls

This classic dish is deliciously low carb with TLC bake mix simply substituted for a high carb one...

12 oz. spicy pork sausage
1-1/2 cups shredded cheddar cheese
3/4 cup TLC Bake mix (plain garbanzo or other whole grain flour is very good here also, in place of the bake mix)
1 Tb. parsley, dried
1-1/2 tsp. garlic powder
1 tsp. sage, ground

Mix ingredients as you would a meatloaf. Form 18 even balls (divide meat into 3 equal portions, then divide each portion into 6 balls). Bake on broiler rack in 350 F oven for 25-30 minutes.

Each: 123 cal, 10 g fat (8 g sat.), 1 g carb, 6 g protein

Wings

Buffalo (hot chicken) wings are one of the most popular items I can think of that are inherently low carb without requiring any adjustment, but that is only one of the many delicious ways to enjoy them!

No matter your preference on the final flavoring, the first step is to wash, dry, season with salt and pepper, and then cook the wings thoroughly. My preferred method is to bake them, because of the ease. I allow 70-80 minutes on a lightly greased broiler rack, at 325-350 F. You can also deep-fry them 1 lb. at a time, frozen, for 15-18 minutes per batch, or just grill them (We like our wings extra-crispy; adjust all cooking times to your preference.)

After cooking, drain briefly on clean toweling if needed, then toss in one of the following sauces. I like to make all the sauces and serve them on the table with oodles of plain wings, because it is so fun for everyone to mix and match and season as they go.

TIP - This is ever-popular party fare, and you can make it all ahead of time. Just reheat the wings as you serve them.

Measurements listed should be enough for 8-12 cooked wing pieces; if making more, increase sauce amounts as needed.

<u>CLASSIC BUFFALO</u>: 3 Tb. melted butter mixed with 1/3 cup Frank's Redhot™ or similar wing-style sauce. At my house, we like to add some hot diced peppers or extra hot sauce of another type and also reduce the butter a little, for some extra kick. I also use this as a grilling sauce and marinade for many different kinds of meat. *Per 3 wings: 443 cal, 33 g fat (13 g sat), 0 g carb, 30 g protein*

<u>GARLIC</u>: 1/4 cup olive oil mixed with 1 Tb. garlic powder or fresh crushed garlic and 1/4 tsp. salt. This sauce should be allowed to set for at least 30 minutes before using, so the oil can more uniformly take on the garlic flavor. I think this works best when you place the sauce in a plastic bag along with the wings, seal tightly, then shake to coat.
Per 3 wings: 464 cal, 37 g fat (8 g sat), <1 g carb, 30 g protein

<u>HONEY MUSTARD</u>: 1/3 cup yellow or Dijon mustard mixed with 2 Tb. oil, 1 Tb. hot water, and 1/3 cup Splenda or equivalent other sweetener. (Don't reserve this one just for wings - it is excellent with and on lots of foods, especially ham.)
Per 3 wings: 368 cal, 25 g fat (6 g sat), 1 g carb, 30 g protein

<u>SWEET & SOUR</u>: 1/4 cup low carb jam or jelly mixed with 2 Tb. each: oil and vinegar. Taste will vary depending on the jam used, but our various results to date have always been delicious! This is another sauce that has many uses. Try it as a grilling sauce, in stir fries, etc.
Per 3 wings: 499 cal, 39 g fat (8 g sat), 1 g carb, 30 g protein

Cheese Sauce TLC

I rarely reach for any sort of thickener these days, which means my cheese sauces have changed a little. These are my current favorites. I think they all cook best in a large non-stick skillet, using a heat-proof rubber spatula. Add ingredients to the pan in the order listed, stirring constantly, and try not to allow any of the sauces to boil, which can cause separation. Quick and versatile, use these sauces over meats, vegetables, in soups, casseroles, etc.

Alfredo
2 Tb. butter
4 Tb. heavy cream
2 oz. cream cheese, diced
4 Tb. grated Parmesan cheese
Per 1/4 cup: 238 cal, 24 g fat (14 g sat), 1 g carb, 5 g protein

Bleu
1/3 cup half and half cream
2 oz. cream cheese, diced
2 oz. bleu cheese, crumbled
1 tsp. cracked black pepper
1 tsp. garlic powder
Yield 2/3 cup - per 1/3 cup: 154 cal, 14 g fat (8 g sat), 2 g carb, 5 g protein

Cheddar
1/3 cup half and half cream
3 oz. cream cheese, diced
1/2 cup shredded sharp cheddar cheese
Dash or two of hot pepper sauce
Yield 3/4 cup - per 1/4 cup: 206 cal, 19 g fat (12 g sat), 2 g carb, 6 g protein

Chili Pepper
1/3 cup half and half cream
3 oz. cream cheese, diced
2 oz. shredded pepper-jack cheese (1/2 cup)
Hot pepper sauce or minced jalapenos to taste
Per 1/4 cup: 277 cal, 26 g fat (15 g sat), 3 g carb, 9 g protein

Cranberry Sauce

4 cups whole cranberries, fresh or frozen
2/3 cup water
2 cups granular Splenda™
2 tsp. dried grated orange peel (or 2 Tb. fresh zest)
Place berries and water in medium saucepan and bring to a boil. Cover, reduce heat, and simmer until berries burst. Stir often to prevent scorching. Remove from heat and stir in orange peel and Splenda.
Makes 3 cups - Per 2 Tb: 20 cal, 0.1 g fat, 4 g carb
VARIATION: Replace water with sugar free syrup and reduce Splenda to 1 cup. *Deduct 1 carb per srv.*

Dilly Lemon Sauce

3 oz. cream cheese
2 Tb. half-and-half cream
2 Tb. lemon juice
2 Tb. chopped fresh dill weed
Salt and pepper to taste
Cube cream cheese and melt slowly with cream over medium-low heat, stirring, until smooth. Add remaining ingredients, taste, and adjust seasonings if necessary. If you really enjoy lemon, add some zest as well as the juice. This sauce is excellent over fish, poultry, vegetables, etc.
Yield 1/2 cup - per 2 Tb: 85 cal, 8 g fat (5 g sat), 1 g carb, 1 g protein

VARIATIONS: Use different herbs, or omit for a plain lemon sauce. Add white wine in place of lemon juice.

Did you know ...

To reduce liquids and make sauces, use a pan with a large surface area such a 10-12 inch non-stick skillet. Smaller, deeper pans take much longer to achieve the same effect.

Dry Rub & Seasoning Mixes

If you can find seasoning mixes without added sugars or MSG that you like, by all means use them. If you can't, it is very easy to make up your own blends. Just mix them well and store them airtight.

ALL-PURPOSE GARLIC & HERB SEASONING
4 Tb. black pepper (you may prefer less)
2 Tb. seasoned salt
2 Tb. dry parsley
2 Tb. paprika
1 Tb. garlic powder
1 Tb. onion powder
1 Tb. ground cumin
Per 1 Tb: 16 cal, 4 g carb
Excellent on and in everything.

SPICY CAJUN SEASONING
1/2 cup paprika
4 Tb. black ground pepper
4 Tb. Garlic powder
2 Tb. onion powder
1 Tb. cayenne pepper
Per 1 Tb: 19 cal, 0.5 g fat, 4 g carb (1 g fiber)
Makes an excellent base for barbecue. To blacken fish or meat, dip in melted butter first, then encrust with Cajun seasoning and sear at a very high heat. After searing, reduce temperature of pan or grill and finish cooking through slowly.

GREEK SPICE MIX
1 Tb. ground thyme
1 Tb. granular Splenda™
2 Tb. dried rosemary
2 Tb. dried lemon peel
2 Tb. dried basil
1/4 cup paprika
Per 1 Tb: 12 cal, <0.5 g fat, 2 g carb
Excellent with lamb, pork, and poultry.

ITALIAN SEASONING MIX
1/2 tsp. ground thyme
1 tsp. dried marjoram
1 tsp. onion powder
1 tsp. ground oregano
2 tsp. cracked pepper
2 tsp. ground basil
2 tsp. celery salt
1 Tb. dried onion flakes
1 Tb. garlic powder
3 Tb. dried parsley
1/3 cup grated dry Parmesan cheese
Per 1 Tb: 12 cal, 0.5 g fat, 1 g carb
For a dressing, mix 3 Tb. dry mix with 3 Tb. vinegar
and 1/2 cup oil. *Per 2 Tb. dressing: 166 cal, 18 g fat
(2 g sat), <1 g carb*

ORANGE-ROSEMARY RUB
1/3 cup granular Splenda™
2 tsp. ground rosemary
1 tsp. garlic powder
1 tsp. salt
Orange extract - add one drop at a time until the
mixture resembles wet sand. Oil the entrée lightly
then rub mix over all outside surfaces before cooking. (For a very large item, you may need to double
or triple these amounts.)
Entire batch: 49 cal, 0.5 g fat, 11 g carb

Hollandaise Sauce
1/2 cup butter
3 egg yolks
2 Tb. lemon juice
1/4 tsp. dry mustard
1/4 tsp. salt
1/4 tsp. white pepper or dash hot pepper sauce
Melt butter until very hot, but not until it turns color.
Place remaining ingredients in a blender and process
until smooth. Add the hot butter <u>very</u> slowly, with
machine running, until thickened. Add some hot water if it gets too thick. *Yield: 1 cup - per 2 Tb: 126
cal, 13 g fat (7 g sat), 0 g carb, 1 g protein*

Jam & Jelly TLC

Absolutely anyone - and by that, I mean YOU - can make traditional, "canned-off" jam or jelly. *Even if you skip the canning part!*

You will need:
- pint or half pint jars, complete with new sealing flats and rings - You can reuse jars and rings, but should always buy new sealing flats
- a large water-bath canner with rack - second hand stores are a great place to find these inexpensively, and complete new canning setups can be purchased for less than $30 US
- large mouth funnel, jar lifter, ladle, lid lifter (has a magnet on the end to pluck flats out of the hot water easily) heat-proof stirring and scraping utensils, and clean towels - you can improvise to do without most of these, if you want
- No sugar needed fruit pectin (I use Ball™ brand)

Step 1: Prepare the fruit and jars
Wash all jars, lids, and rings well. If making jelly, sterilize jars according to the instructions and times included in the pectin.

Fill a clean canner halfway with warm water, and keep jars and lids warm in the water on low heat while preparing the jam. I put the flats in a smaller pan of water and balance that on top of the jars, to make it easy to find the flats when needed. Put the cover on and let this go on low heat until you are ready to fill the jars.

Choosing good fruit is important. Do not use bruised, over-ripe, or under-ripe specimens. Wash and sort well, and peel if necessary. To peel fruits for jam such as plums or peaches, I use the same technique as when peeling tomatoes: Cut a small x in the skin, then lower into rapidly boiling water for one minute. Remove from boiling water; drop into a bowl of ice water to instantly halt the cooking process. When cool enough to handle, the skins will slip right off! Chop or crush large berries and fruits into smaller pieces to make jams. To make jelly with wild berries and fruits such as crabapple and chokecherries (two things I love to mix with rhubarb) add enough water to cover the clean fruit completely, boil until soft, then put the mixture through a food mill or strainer of some kind to remove pits, skin, etc. You'll have to guess at the measurements when working with wild produce, but that's half the fun of it. I have had great luck using the proportions as listed by Ball for apple juice jelly but substituting any manner of fruit extract, diluted with sugar free syrups to reduce carbs. I often cook down the fruit down into juice one day, and then make and can the actual jelly the following day - or even the following week... (the plain juice will hold in the refrigerator for a while). The preservatives in sugar free syrups will make your homemade jams last longer.

Step 2: Add ingredients, then boil with pectin

Measure the fruit juice or pulp and place it in a large, deep, non-reactive pan. Add water, sweetener, sugar free syrup, or flavorings as desired. Use the guide that comes inside the pectin and the recipes that follow for measurement guidelines. You should taste each mixture for yourself at this point, and adjust the sweetening as needed. Add the pectin slowly over medium heat, stirring constantly; bring to a full rolling boil. Boil and stir for exactly one minute, then remove from heat and allow to rest for a few minutes, during which time some foam will rise to the top as shown. (Some mixtures will foam a LOT, and others will foam only a little.)

Step 3: Remove any foam

Use a spoon to carefully skim all the foam off the jam or jelly. DO NOT SKIP THIS STEP, or your end product will be very unappealing. It may seem wasteful to discard a cup or more of foam, but it beats ruining the whole batch. Trust me.

Step 4: Fill the jars

Remove the warm jars from the canner and drain briefly. Fill the jars with the hot skimmed jam, one at a time, then place each in the canner. Fill jars to within one quarter inch from the top of the jar; do not overfill (some "head space" is required.) BEFORE ADDING A SEALING FLAT, WIPE THE TOP LIP OF THE JAR AND THE THREADS WITH A CLEAN DAMP TOWEL, TO INSURE THAT THESE AREAS ARE COMPLETELY CLEAN. Center the warm sealing flat on the jar and hand-tighten the jar ring. Do not attempt to over-tighten; the actual seal comes from the canning process.

Step 5: Process (seal) the jars in a hot water bath

Position the canning rack at the top of the canner using the built-in "hooks" and place each jar in rack as they are filled. Do not over-fill the canner; jars should never be stacked on top of each other in a water bath canner, and there should be room for water to circulate in between each jar. When the filled jars are arranged in the rack, slowly lower it to the bottom. Jars should be completely immersed in water and covered by at least one to two inches of water - add additional warm water at this point if you need to bring the water level up. Increase heat to high, and bring the water in the canner to a full rolling boil. Start timing only after the boil starts. Process the jars according to the chart in the pectin. Processing times differ for jellies and jams and it is always best to go over than under.

Step 6: Clean and inspect the jars

After processing is complete, remove jars from the canner and place on a towel or rack to cool. The actual seal occurs as they cool, so do not be alarmed if some do not appear to be thoroughly sealed when first removed from the water bath. Once the jars are cool, inspect each one for a tight seal and immediately refrigerate any that are not secure, or reprocess with a new flat. Affix a colorful label, if desired. If you processed the jars for a long time or have very hard water, a build up of chalky minerals may cloud the jars and lids. Use a paper towel dampened with white vinegar to clean this off.

I always fill one regular container to be placed immediately in the refrigerator and consumed (I don't bother to process this jam in the canner at all.) There is no real need to "can off" *any* homemade jam or jelly, ever - if you want, just make half batches regularly instead. Make jam and put it right in the refrigerator, where it will keep well for two to three weeks. You can even process the jelly juice in bulk when harvesting in season, then measure and freeze that in just the right amounts for single or half batches. When you are ready to make another batch, it will be easy to thaw and use just what you need.

Here are some suggestions for making jams with traditional fruits, and the estimated carb counts based on the actual weights, measurements, and yields obtained by me. *Please note that your actual results may vary, and in fact, results can vary from batch to batch due to differences in fruit.*

Strawberry-Rhubarb Jam
1/2 lb. frozen or fresh whole strawberries
1/2 lb. frozen or fresh rhubarb, chopped
Cook down and crush fruit. Add 2 Tb. lemon juice and additional sugar free syrup as needed to measure 5 cups total. Add 1 box pectin according to guidelines given. *Yield: 5 cups - per 2 Tb: 9 cal, 2 g carb*

Peach Jam
12 large fresh peaches, peeled & crushed - Add 1/4 cup lemon juice and peach flavored sugar free syrup as needed to measure 5 cups total. Add 1 box pectin according to guidelines given. *Yield: 5 cups - per 2 Tb: 11 cal, <3 g carb*

Blueberry Jam
1 quart fresh or frozen crushed blueberries and 2 Tb. lemon juice plus sugar free syrup as needed to measure 5 cups total. Add 1 box pectin according to guidelines given. *Yield: 5 cups - per 2 Tb: 14 cal, 3 g carb*

Instant Fruit Jam

1 cup dried unsweetened cranberries
1 cup very hot sugar free syrup (pick your flavor)
1-1/2 tsp. guar gum or 1-1/2 Tb. Notstarch™
Simply combine these ingredients in a good blender and pulse until combined and slightly thickened. Chill and enjoy! *Makes 1 cup - per 2 Tb: 16 cal, 4 g carb*

World's Easiest Refrigerator Jam

5 cups chopped low carb fruit or berries (no citrus)
2 cups granular Splenda™
3 oz. pkg. SF gelatin (any complimentary flavor)
Mix fruit and Splenda together in a large saucepan, cover, and leave at room temperature for several hours or overnight. Bring to a boil over medium heat and continue to boil for 6 minutes, stirring constantly to prevent scorching. Remove from heat and stir in gelatin (dry mix only, unprepared). Cool slightly before placing jam in clean containers and refrigerating.
Experiment with fun combinations like cherry gelatin and rhubarb, orange gelatin with peaches, or strawberries with raspberry gelatin, etc. If you find you like your jam a little looser, or want to make syrup instead, add 1/4 to 1/2 cup sugar free syrup next time. Take notes as you go and create your very own signature jams and syrups - it's a blast!
Carbs will vary a lot depending on combinations used, and actual yield, which can very from batch to batch depending on fruit ripeness and other factors, but here are some examples for jam:
Made with 5 average peaches or 5 cups strawberries or raspberries, figuring yield of 3 cups - *per 2 Tb: 28 cal, 5 g carb, 2 g protein*
Rhubarb - *deduct 1 carb per serving*
Whole cranberries - *add 1 carb per serving*
Blueberries - *add 2 g carb per serving*

Salad Dressings

BACON MUSTARD

8 thick slices bacon, diced (4 oz.)
1/3 cup diced onion
2 tsp. guar gum or 2 Tb. ThickenThin Notstarch™
1 cup water
1/2 cup cider vinegar
1/2 cup granular Splenda™
1 Tb. Dijon mustard
1/2 tsp. each: salt and pepper
Tabasco™ sauce to taste

Fry bacon until crisp; remove from pan; reserve. Discard all but 2 Tb. of grease from the pan. Add onion and sauté until dark (caramelized). Sprinkle starch over onions slowly, stirring constantly. Add remaining ingredients in order listed, then add back bacon bits. *Makes 2 cups - per 2 Tb: 51 cal, 5 g fat (1 g sat), 1 g carb*

CREAMY GARLIC

1 cup mayonnaise
3 Tb. grated Parmesan cheese
3 Tb. lemon juice
3 Tb. half and half cream
2 Tb. garlic (roasted or minced)
2 tsp. cracked pepper
2 tsp. granular Splenda™
1/2 tsp. salt

Just whisk it all together! Best after resting for several hours. *Makes 1-2/3 cups - per 2 Tb: 191 cal, 18 g fat (2 g sat) 2 g carb, 1 g protein*

FRENCH

1/3 cup tomato paste
1/2 cup warm water
1/2 cup granular Splenda™
1 tsp. salt
3/4 cup oil
1/4 cup white vinegar

Add everything but oil and vinegar to a blender and puree. Add oil very slowly, then add vinegar last. *Makes 2 cups - per 2 Tb: 96 cal, 10 g fat (1 g sat), 1 g carb*

Schmears

Beat these versatile mixes till well-mixed and fluffy. I use my food processor most often, but if ingredients are at room temperature, they are easy to mix by hand, too. Try them on fruit, vegetables, low carb toast, bagels, tortillas, crackers, etc.

MORNING
4 oz. cream cheese, softened
1/2 cup cottage cheese
2-3 Tb. SF vanilla syrup
1 Tb. vanilla protein powder
Makes 3/4 cup - per 2 Tb: 87 cal, 7 g fat (4 sat), 1 g carb, 3 g protein

CINNAMON
Follow above recipe but add 1 tsp. ground cinnamon and 1/3 cup sweetener in place of the sugar free syrup. I often add finely chopped, toasted nuts to this one. *Per 2 Tb: 94 cal, 7 g fat (4 sat), 2 g carb, 3 g protein*

GARLIC & HERB
8 oz. cream cheese, softened
2/3 cup mayonnaise
1/2 cup crumbled feta cheese
1/2 cup grated Parmesan cheese
1 Tb. garlic (powder, roasted, or minced)
2 Tb. dry parsley
Tastes okay on day 1 and 2, but on Day 3 something wondrous happens. If eating right away, I recommend using the garlic powder. If able to allow it to set before eating, then minced garlic is best here. *Makes 1-1/2 cups - per 2 Tb: 224 cal, 21 g fat (7 g sat), 1 g carb, 4 g protein*

"HONEY" NUT BUTTER
1/2 cup creamy style unsweetened peanut butter
3 Tb. butter, softened
3 Tb. SF syrup (I prefer French vanilla, but you can use almost any flavor with good results.
Makes 3/4 cup - per 2 Tb: 215 cal, 19 g fat (5 sat), 6 g carb (1 g fiber), 6 g protein

Vanilla Extract

For good results, you will need to spend some money on high-quality, very aromatic vanilla beans. When you cut them, they should seem moist inside, slick outside, and be pliable enough to bend in half without breaking. The next ingredient is high-quality vodka. Traditional vanilla extracts may be made with bourbon, but we don't have years for this project, so take a shortcut and substitute Absolut™ or another decent vodka - don't break the bank, but don't use "well", liquor either. Next, you need a small glass bottle to age the mixture in. Dark glass would be best, but if you're storing it in a dark cupboard anyway, it really doesn't matter if you use clear or dark glass. A metal flask would be fine, as well, but I like being able to see inside once in a while. Don't use plastic, since the alcohol could leach chemicals out of the plastic and into the extract, over time. Quantities are subjective - I used about 1-1/2 cups of vodka to 2 full-size vanilla beans (each about 12"-14" long) and I was happy with the end result after 4 months, but I am happier yet after 7 months. If your beans are not the best, you may need to use more of them, and/or wait even longer for good flavor. This is not a weekend project, but it will only take a few minutes of your time now, and you'll be glad later, since most commercial vanilla extracts do contain unnecessary and unwanted sugar. Lay the beans on a cutting surface and use a sharp knife to split them in half, the long way, exposing the seeds inside. Then just cut them into shorter lengths, drop them in the container, cover them with vodka, close it tightly, set it in a dark place without extremes in temperature and ..... wait! That's all. I can't tell you how long it is 'safe' to keep using this mixture, for sure, but mine just keeps getting better and better. Occasionally I remove a small amount to use over the next couple of months, then add more vodka to the bottle. Strain the vanilla through a bit of cheesecloth or fine mesh when removing for your own use, or before giving as gifts.

I count this like pure vodka: per Tb: 32 cal, 0 carbs

Yogurt TLC

"Yogurt? you say.... What's this about yogurt? I thought we couldn't eat yogurt anymore!"

So began my quest... some people on an internet message board where I participated were talking about a "yogurt exception". Eventually I found myself reading *"GO-Diet" by Jack Goldberg, Ph.D. and Karen O'Mara, D.O., (Go Corp.; June 1999; ISBN 0967084601),* where I found credible, scientific testimony detailing the discrepancy between the carbs listed on the label for plain yogurt and its actual carb count. These doctors advise (based on actual lab tests that they performed) in the case of cultured milk products, to not count the carbohydrates as stated on the package labels, but instead to count yogurt, buttermilk, and kefir at just 4 carbs per cup.

Yogurt is an excellent source of calcium, riboflavin (B2) and protein. Thanks to its naturally acidic nature, it can help baked goods to rise - used in place of some or all of the specified liquid in cakes, muffins, pancakes, etc., you can actually reduce the amount of baking powder you need. If you find some of the low carb homemade ice cream recipes a tad on the heavy side (sometimes they leave an actual coating on the roof of your mouth), try using yogurt for half the cream called for, the next time. Homemade yogurt "cheese" (strain yogurt in a fine sieve/coffee filter placed over a catch bowl for a day to remove the whey) makes an excellent substitution for cream cheese in recipes. Yogurt is a delicious addition to protein shakes (more like smoothies then) and egg dishes, it's great by the spoonful once you add some sweetener, and some fruit and/or extracts as flavoring, or you can add sugar free syrup (tends to thin it down - adding some protein powder, pectin, or gelatin can help to mitigate that). I like to eat it with small amounts of whole grain cereals for crunch. Yogurt is also a great medium for ground flax seeds, nuts, coconut, etc.... get creative! Freeze doctored up yogurt in Popsicle molds for a cool and tasty treat on a hot afternoon.... make luscious cucumber dips, creamy dressings...

you get the picture!

I found lots of different methods for making yogurt when I started researching this matter, and quite a bit of conflicting information, but one thing that everyone seemed to agree on was this: the first step is to heat whatever milk mixture you decide to use, to the boiling point. Heating the milk to boiling kills any undesirable bacteria that might be present, which is always a good thing, even in this age of ultra pasteurized store-bought products - because hey, you just never know who's going to screw up on any given day, and safe always beats sorry! The scalding process also changes the properties of the milk proteins in such a way that the yogurt attains a denser, firmer texture than it could otherwise, helping the whey to not separate easily from the finished product and giving your yogurt a longer shelf life.

After heating the milk to boiling, it should be allowed to cool until it reaches the optimum incubation temperature of 110 F (43.3 C), at which time you add yogurt "starter" consisting of live bacteria. Yogurt starter can be purchased as dry granules (check health food stores) or you can just use plain yogurt from the grocery store, any kind that isn't sweetened or flavored and also says "contains live cultures" (plain Yoplait™ or Dannon™ both work well.) You can use your own yogurt from a preceding batch as starter, once you get this process going, but bacteria do become less active with age, so the older the yogurt is that you use for starter, the more of it you will need to use. It's never a problem to add more, you can't add too much, so I am always generous with the amount when using homemade yogurt as my starter.

You'll need a good thermometer to make good yogurt, since adding the starter at the proper temperature is crucial to your success. Temperatures above 115 degrees F (46.1 C) cause separation and curdling and can destroy the active yogurt culture, while temperatures below 100 degrees F (37.8 C) stop their growth. The longer yogurt is allowed to incubate, the thicker it will become. It takes at least four hours for a good "set", but I like mine best after ten to fourteen hours of incubation.

You can incubate yogurt in a commercial yogurt maker, making the whole process completely foolproof and worry-free. If you have any issues with an impaired immune system or you could be pregnant, then you won't want to take any chances, and you should <u>only</u> use a controlled system. But... if you don't have any issues like that, you can employ a number of different methods for the actual incubation, ranging from an old heating pad lined with towels to a styrofoam cooler filled with a heating pad and packing peanuts to an electric fry-pan filled with warm water to a sunny windowsill to an oven with a lit pilot light to .... a good ole' fashioned metal thermos, which is how I do it. Don't use a plastic or otherwise cheap thermos - you really need a good metal or glass thermos that holds heat for a long time. Fill the thermos with BOILING water, screw on the lid, and allow it to preheat while your scalded milk mixture is cooling down to 110 F. Once the scalded milk has cooled, stir in the starter. Dump the water from the thermos, put the milk/starter mix in the thermos, screw on the lid, and leave it alone for 4 hours and 30 minutes. Don't open or check or even MOVE it meanwhile, because you don't want to reduce the temperature too much, and too much jostling can actually disturb the bacterial action and affect the final product. After 4-1/2 hours, open it up and you should have yogurt. Take it out, put it in something else (single serving sized plastic dishes are great for this) stick it in the fridge, then once it's chilled, enjoy it! If you find it's not thick enough for you with this short of an incubation period, which was the case with me, you can dissolve 1 tsp. plain gelatin or some fruit pectin in the milk while scalding it. (The thermos will only hold the yogurt at an incubation temperature for a few hours, after which the thickening action is also halted no matter how long you leave it out, so this is the only way I could think of to make yogurt as thick with the thermos method as with my machine. You can also use this method to make yogurt which is incubated in a machine thicker than it would be otherwise. I recommend making it plain first, and adjusting subsequent batches.

To use any of the incubators, do this: (if you find one used and cheap, without directions, don't hesitate to BUY IT, because they all work the same way.)
1] scald the milk mixture you've decide to use (the quantity will depend on the size of your machine, and the recipe is up to you - more on that in a moment)
2] cool it down to precisely 110 Fahrenheit (43.3 Celsius)
3] skim off or stir in the skin that will have formed while it cooled
4] add starter medium of your choice
5] place it in the machine in containers, and close covers (if needed, you can use baby food, canning or condiment jars in place of the jars that come standard with most incubators, whatever fits.)
6] turn on the machine and "let it rip" for the desired number of hours (I like ten. I start a batch, go to bed, then when I get up the next day, it's ready. Easy! Anywhere from 3 to 14 hrs. is considered 'normal' - you'll have to experiment and see what you prefer.)

My preferred milk mixture:
3 cups whole milk
2/3 cup heavy cream
1/3 - 1/2 cup yogurt or 1 envelope starter
Makes 4 cups - per half cup, with no adjustments to carbs: *129 cal, 10 g fat (6 g sat), 5 g carb*, 3 g protein*

*If you agree with the yogurt "exception" described earlier, you can count this item as only 2 carbs, but rest assured that recipes in this book that call for yogurt have been analyzed to include all of the carbs in the yogurt, without revision of any kind.

Baked Beans

2 cans black soy beans, 15 oz. each (3-1/2 cups)
1/2 cup real bacon bits (or chopped ham)
1/2 cup chopped onion
1/2 cup tomato sauce
3 Tb. yellow mustard
1/2 cup granular Splenda™

Drain and rinse beans well. Combine remaining ingredients and cook slowly for as long as you want. I like to use a crockpot (slow cooker) on low for at least six hours.

Makes about 4 cups - per 1/2 cup: 209 cal, 10 g fat (3 g sat), 10 g carb (6 g fiber), 18 g protein

Best Thing Since Scalloped Potatoes

6 cups sliced celery root, a.k.a. celeriac (or turnips)
1 cup mayonnaise
1/2 cup buttermilk
1/2 cup bacon bits (real, not imitation)
2 Tb. dry onion flakes
1 tsp. black pepper
1/2 cup grated Parmesan cheese

Add sliced roots to already-boiling, salted water and simmer just till fork-tender, about 15 minutes depending on thickness. Drain and pat dry. Preheat oven to 350 F. Grease a shallow baking dish and arrange cooked slices in the pan. Whisk together mayonnaise and buttermilk; pour over slices. Sprinkle bacon bits, onion flakes, pepper, and Parmesan over all. Bake for 40-45 minutes, until golden brown. Allow to stand at room temp. for five minutes before serving. *Yield: 8 servings*

Made with celery root: *435 cal, 34 g fat (8 g sat), 9 g carb, 12 g protein, each*

Made with turnips: *425 cal, 34 g fat (8 g sat), 7 g carb (2 g fiber), 12 g protein, each*

Celery Root Rémoulade

3/4 cup buttermilk
2 tsp. ThickenThin NotStarch™ or 3/4 tsp. guar gum
1/2 tsp. salt
Pinch of cayenne pepper or dash pepper sauce
1 egg yolk
2 tsp. olive oil
2 tsp. parsley
2 tsp. tarragon
1 Tb. drained capers, rinsed
1 anchovy fillet, chopped
1 tsp. grated onion or shallot
1 tsp. brown mustard
1 tsp. granular Splenda™
1 Tb. lemon juice
1 lb. celeriac (about 2 cups, once shredded)

Whisk 1/4 cup of the buttermilk with the starch, salt, and pepper in a saucepan. Blend in the egg yolk, then add remaining buttermilk. Simmer over moderate heat, stirring constantly, until the mixture thickens, about five minutes. Transfer to a small bowl, and gradually whisk in the oil, herbs, capers, onion, anchovy, mustard, Splenda, and lemon juice. Chill, covered, at least thirty minutes. Just before you are ready to serve, peel and shred or grate the celery root and toss it with the chilled sauce.

Makes six servings - per each: 74 calories, 3 g fat (0 sat), 9 g carb (1 g fiber), 3 g protein.

Did you know...

Celeriac is not actually the root of the celery which we regularly eat, but is instead a special variety of celery, developed especially for its large root by gardeners in Northern Europe and the Mediterranean as far back as the Renaissance period.

Celery and celeriac are known for having anti-inflammatory properties, and are often recommended for people with arthritis or rheumatism.

Chayote Rellanos

4 medium chayote squash, about 8 oz. each
1 tsp. salt and 6-8 cups water, for boiling
3 slices TLC light oat bread
2 cups shredded sharp Cheddar cheese, divided
1 cup grated Parmesan cheese, divided
1/4 cup wheat bran
1 egg, lightly beaten
2 tsp. crushed fresh garlic or garlic powder
1/4 cup green onions, thinly sliced
1/4 tsp. cayenne pepper or dash hot pepper sauce
1/2 tsp. black pepper
1/2 tsp. celery salt

Cut the chayotes in half the long way. Place in a saucepan and cover with one inch of water. Add salt, bring to a boil, and simmer for about 15 minutes, until tender. Remove from saucepan and immerse in ice water for a few minutes, to halt the cooking process. Preheat oven to 425 F. Pat cooled chayote halves dry with a clean or paper towel, and remove the seeds. Using a spoon, melon baller, etc., remove the flesh from each half, leaving a thin shell intact. Set the shells aside. Shred the bread into soft crumbs. Dice the chayote flesh (you should have around 2 cups) and combine it with the bread crumbs, 1-1/2 cups of the cheddar cheese, 3/4 cup of the Parmesan, the bran, egg, garlic, onions, cayenne pepper or sauce, celery salt, and pepper. Divide the resulting filling mixture evenly between the reserved shells, packing it gently but firmly into the shells, and mounding the filling up and smoothing it over as needed. Combine the remaining cheddar cheese with the remaining Parmesan. Cover the filling with this mixture, pushing it into the filling lightly if needed, to make it stick. Arrange the stuffed squash in a greased baking dish and bake for 20-25 minutes, until hot throughout and golden brown on top.

Makes 8 servings - per each: 229 cal, 15 g fat (9 g sat), 9 g carb (1 g fiber), 14 g protein, each.

Frosted Cauliflower

1 large head cauliflower or 2 small (about 3 pounds)
1 cup sour cream
1/3 cup mayonnaise
1/3 cup yellow mustard
2 tsp. paprika
1/2 tsp. each: salt and pepper

This is tasty, versatile, and a great way to disguise any older heads of cauliflower that need to be "shaved" before eating. You can prepare it ahead of time, and then just pop the casserole dish in the oven at the last minute.

Remove the core from the cleaned cauliflower, then boil or steam the head, whole, until almost done. Drain well, and place upright in a baking dish. Whisk sour cream, mayo, and mustard; pour over cauliflower. Sprinkle with spices, then bake uncovered until cooked through and hot - 20-30 minutes at 350 F. When cooking other foods at other temperatures, simply adjust baking times as needed. To serve, slice in 6 equal wedges; spoon mustard sauce over top.

Makes about 6 cups - per 1-cup wedge: 234 cal, 21 g fat (6 g sat), 7 g carb (3 g fiber), 3 g protein.

Did you know...

The chayote (pronounced "chi-OH-tay") differs from other summer squash because of its large central seed and thick, deeply ridged skin. Chayote look a little like patty pan squash, but are about the size and shape of a large pear, with pale green skin and light flesh.

One cup of boiled or steamed unseasoned chayote squash has 38 calories, 1 gram protein, 1 gram fat, and 8 grams carbohydrate. The chayote squash is a great source of potassium (276 milligrams per cup) and has some vitamin C, too.

Lemon-Dill Daikon

2 cups peeled, sliced daikon radish (about 6 oz.)
1 Tb. oil
1 tsp. granular Splenda™
1/4 tsp. salt
1/4 tsp. white or black pepper
1 Tb. minced fresh parsley or 1.5 tsp. dried
2 tsp. minced fresh dill weed or 1 tsp. dried
juice and grated peel from 1/2 small lemon
Heat oil in a large skillet. Add sliced daikon and toss to coat. Add Splenda, salt, and pepper. Toss over moderately high heat until daikon is tender-crisp, about 5 minutes. Remove to serving dish; toss with parsley, dill, and lemon and serve immediately.
Makes about 2 cups - per half-cup: 40 calories, 3.5 g fat (0 sat), 2 g carb, each
VARIATIONS: Substitue jicama for daikon. *Per serving: 51 cal, 3 g fat, 4 g carb, 1 g protein.* May also substitute other herbs for dill - I am personally partial to cilantro, and I then like to add 2-3 fresh jalapenos or serrano peppers, as well. (Cook them with the roots. Spicy good!)

Nutty Spinach

12 oz. fresh spinach leaves, well washed and dried
1/2 cup sliced almonds
2 Tb. oil
1 tsp. minced garlic
1 tsp. balsamic vinegar
1 tsp. salt
1/4 tsp. black pepper (or chili pepper flakes)
Add oil to hot pan, followed by nuts and garlic. Cook for one minute, then add spinach leaves, vinegar, salt and pepper (if using chili flakes, add those at the beginning instead, with the nuts and garlic). Turn and cook JUST until the leaves wilt and turn bright green. Serve immediately.
Makes about 4 cups - per 1 cup: 156 cal, 14 g fat (1 g sat), 5 g carb (3 g fiber), 4 g protein

Oriental Vegetable Medley

2 Tb. oil
6 green onions, sliced diagonally (including greens, 1 cup total)
1 medium red bell pepper, seeded and chopped
4 stalks celery, sliced (about 1/2 cup)
1 medium carrot, peeled and sliced diagonally (1/2 cup)
2 tsp. fresh grated ginger root
1/4 cup soy sauce or liquid aminos
1/2 cup sliced water chestnuts, drained (small can)
1/2 cup fresh sliced white mushrooms
1/2 bunch broccoli, in florets (about 3 cups, or 10 oz. frozen)

Add oil to a hot pan, followed by prepared vegetables. Cook and stir, uncovered, for about 5 minutes. Add ginger root, soy sauce, and salt and pepper to taste, then cover and allow to steam for a few minutes longer, until tender-crisp or as desired.

Makes 4 cups - per cup: 151 cal, 7.5 g fat (0 g sat), 16 g carb (6 g fiber), 7 g protein

VARIATION: Omit the carrot and you may deduct 8 calories and 2 carbs per serving.

Parmesan Garlic Zucchini

2 medium zucchini (I mean store-sized medium squash, not home-grown garden monsters - about 600 g or 1.25 lb., cleaned)
2 Tb. oil
3 Tb. butter
1/2 tsp. minced garlic
2 Tb. Parmesan cheese
1 tsp. salt
1/2 - 1 tsp. black pepper

Slice squash into bite-size pieces. Add oil and butter to hot pan, followed by squash. Cook and toss until squash is tender-crisp. Add garlic for the last two minutes of cooking only. Just before serving, add cheese and spices.

Yield 4 cups - per 1 cup: 170 cal, 16 g fat (6 g sat), 4 g carb (1 g fiber), 2 g protein

Rice TLC

Grated cauliflower makes a *magnificent* stand-in for rice! Simply grate fresh cauliflower, and cook it by any means desired, using it wherever you would have used rice in the past. I use a large Cuisinart™ for this task and do not recommend trying to do this by hand or with an inferior machine. There will always be some small pieces that do not grate completely, and which can be removed.

As always, I weighed and measured personally in order to arrive at a carb count for this item. I have found that a large head of cauliflower that weighs 1250 grams (cleaned) yields 11 cups of grated cauliflower. I prepare two or three at one time, dividing the grated cauliflower into 5-cup portions, which I then freeze. The frozen portions can be used in the following recipes (just adjust your cooking estimates accordingly, add some extra liquid IF needed at the end to complete cooking, and don't allow them to accumulate ice crytals before use - best to vacuum-seal, if possible.) Once cooked, you should get about 4 cups of prepared "rice" for every 5 cups and 1.4 lb. (625 g) of lightly packed raw grated cauliflower that you start with. Using those calculations, *1 cup steamed cauliflower rice is equal to 35 calories, 0.8 g fat, 6 g carb (4 g fiber), and 2 g protein* - an incredible carb bargain!

CURRIED RICE
1 Tb. oil
1/2 cup chopped onion
3/4 cup water
2 tsp. instant chicken bullion granules
2 tsp. garlic powder
1/2 tsp. ground ginger
1/4 tsp. black pepper
5 tsp. curry powder
1-2 Tb. granular Splenda™ (start with one Tb; adjust to taste)
5 cups lightly packed grated raw cauliflower (625 g)
3 Tb. heavy cream
Sauté onion in oil over medium heat, until softened

and translucent but not browned. Add water and bring to boil. Add dry spices and stir until mixed. Add cauliflower and cream; cook and stir uncovered over medium heat while the liquid reduces, until the desired consistency is reached, 20-30 minutes.

Makes about 4 cups - per one cup: 128 calories, 9 g fat (3 g sat), 11 g carb (5 g fiber), 3 g protein

ONE DISH MEAL VARIATION - <u>CHICKEN CURRY</u>:

Increase oil to 3 Tb. Add 2 lb. boneless skinless chicken breast (in bite size pieces) to pan first (you will need a very large one), and brown well on all sides before adding the onion, followed by the mixed dry spices. Replace the water and cream with 2 cups (usually 1 can) coconut milk. *4 servings, each: 544 cal, 33 g fat (15 g sat), 14 g carb (5 g fiber), 53 g protein.*

<u>FRIED RICE</u>

5 cups grated cauliflower (625 g)
1 tsp. salt
2 cups chicken broth
4 stalks celery, sliced
3 Tb. diced pimento
1/3 cup grated onion
1/3 cup soy sauce
2 tsp ground ginger
2 tsp. garlic powder
1 Tb. granular Splenda™
1 Tb. unseasoned rice or white wine vinegar
2 eggs
2 Tb. water

Add grated cauliflower, salt, and chicken broth to large uncovered non-stick skillet over medium heat and boil till cauliflower is very soft and liquid is almost gone, 20-30 minutes. Add vegetables, seasonings, Splenda, and vinegar. When mixture has reduced enough to begin to clump, move to side of pan. Beat eggs with water; add to empty side of pan and allow to cook through (scramble), then stir the cooked eggs into the rice mixture. Continue to cook and stir until proper consistency is attained.

Makes about 6 cups – per 1-1/2 cups: 115 calories, 3 g fat (0 sat), 10 g carb (4 g fiber), 12 g protein

SPANISH RICE

6 oz. bacon, diced (3-4 thick slices)
1/2 cup chopped onion
1/2 cup green pepper, chopped
3 tsp. garlic
2 cups Mexican-style stewed tomatoes (1 avg. can)
1/4 tsp. salt
1/2 tsp. black pepper (adjust to taste)
5 cups grated fresh cauliflower (625 g)

Fry diced bacon until crisp; add onion and continue to cook until softened. Add garlic and cook 1-2 more minutes, then stir in remaining ingredients and continue to cook until liquid evaporates and proper consistency is reached. *Makes 4 cups - per 1 cup: 294 cal, 24 g fat (7 g sat), 13 g carb (5 g fiber), 7 g protein*

WILD RICE MEDLEY

3 Tb. butter, divided
1 Tb. oil
1/2 cup chopped onion
1/4 cup minced celery
1/4 cup chopped fresh mushrooms
2 cups chicken broth (an average can)
1 tsp. garlic powder
1 Tb. dried parsley
3/4-1 tsp. salt
1/2 tsp. black pepper
2 tsp. granular Splenda™
5 cups grated fresh caulilflower
1/2 cup real wild rice (dry, unprepared)

Add 1 Tb. butter and the oil to a hot pan. Sauté onion, celery, and mushrooms until softened. Add remaining ingredients and continue to cook, stirring occasionally, until liquid is reduced, proper consistency is reached, and wild rice is tender. Add additional water if needed. Stir in remaining butter just before serving, and adjust seasonings to taste then. *Makes 6 cups - per 1 cup: 165 cal, 9 g fat (3 g sat), 16 g carb (4 g fiber), 6 g protein*

Squash Delight

Even the pickiest eaters usually enjoy this dish - and rightly so.

2 Tb. oil
6 cups yellow or green zucchini squash, diced
1/2 cup onion, chopped
1/3 cup sour cream
1/3 cup Ranch dressing
1 cup cheddar cheese, shredded
2 Tb. bacon bits
2 Tb. dry onion flakes
1/2 tsp. black pepper

Sauté the squash and onion in the oil for 2-3 minutes, to soften slightly. Do not overcook. Place in a well-greased, shallow casserole dish. Mix sour cream and ranch dressing and toss with vegetables. Cover with cheddar cheese, onion flakes, bacon bits, and black pepper. Bake uncovered at 350 F for about 30 minutes, until golden brown on top and bubbly at edges.

Makes about 6 cups, cooked - per 1 cup: 220 cal, 18 g fat (7 g sat), 8 g carb (1 g fiber), 8 g protein

VARIATION: <u>QUICK GREEN BEAN CASSEROLE</u>
This isn't quite like the old stand-by made with condensed soup and "French fried onions" from a can - it is actually better! Especially when made with fresh steamed beans instead of canned ones.

Substitute cooked green beans for the diced zucchini. Sauté the onion in the oil along with 1 cup sliced fresh mushrooms (instead of the zucchini). Mix this with the beans in the baking dish. Substitute mayonnaise for the Ranch dressing and add 2 tsp. Worcestershire sauce. I prefer to use a white shredded cheese, such as Monterey Jack, in place of cheddar. Omit the bacon bits in the topping and increase the onion flakes to 3 Tb.

Makes 8 cups - per 1 cup : 246 cal, 20 g fat (6 g sat), 10 g carb (1 g fiber), 6 g protein

VARIATION: Replace dry onion flakes with fresh sliced onions fried in butter until dark (caramelized.)

Stuffing TLC

For me, "holiday dinner" means a big meal centered around turkey and dressing (stuffing). Stuffing is one of those things for which I am personally willing to stretch my carb limit temporarily - I can live without the potatoes and winter squash, but I'm just not having turkey without dressing on big days, and that's <u>that</u>!

Before I reached maintenance, I made stuffing with a combination of All-Bran™ extra fiber cereal and pork rinds (see Vol. I), and you can keep carbs very low doing that. If you have low carbohydrate bread, you can make an excellent traditional stuffing by using that in any of your favorite existing recipes, or the following.

COOK TLC STUFFINGS AS FOLLOWS: Bake in a well-greased casserole until heated through, uncovering for the last fifteen to twenty minutes if you like a crunchy top, or use inside a bird, chops, whole fish, rolled roast, etc. If you use it in a bird, allow it to cool before placing it inside the cavity, and make sure both the bird and stuffing reach an internal temperature of 180 F before serving (insert an instant-read thermometer deep inside the stuffing as well as the thigh, to verify safe serving temperatures).

<u>TRADITIONAL BREAD STUFFING</u>
1/2 cup butter
1 cup onion, chopped
2 cups celery, sliced
1 Tb. poultry seasoning
2 Tb. ground sage (or more to taste)
1/2 tsp. salt
1/4 tsp. pepper
2 tsp. marjoram
18 slices TLC light oat bread, cubed and dried
1 egg
Chicken broth or water, as needed
Sauté onion and celery in butter until soft. Add remaining ingredients and toss, tasting and adjusting seasonings prior to adding the egg. Add chicken

broth or water as needed until it just clings together.
*Makes about 8 cups - per 3/4 cup: 276 cal, 18 g fat
(9 g sat), 18 g carb (3 g fiber), 10 g protein*

The following recipes may be a higher in carbs than most of my everyday side dishes, but they're also chock-full of fiber and flavor, meaning I can eat them more often, and not save them just for special occasions.

CRANBERRY-ORANGE DRESSING
My family's favorite! Baked in a casserole dish, this didn't resemble traditional dressing very much, but was still judged "fantastic!" The portion I cooked actually "stuffed" turned out great in both taste and appearance, so I recommend baking this inside the bird or roast, etc., wherever possible.
1/2 cup butter
2 cups sliced green onions, including green ends (about 2 bunches)
2 cups chopped celery
1-1/2 cups pecans, coarsely chopped
1 cup whole cranberries, fresh or frozen
1 tsp. salt
1 tsp. pepper
2 Tb. dry parsley
2-3 tsp. orange extract (must adjust for taste and differences between brands)
2 cups All-Bran™ extra fiber cereal
This recipe makes enough stuffing for an 8-10 pound turkey or boneless rolled beef or pork roast. Half this recipe is suitable for a 3-4 pound rolled roast, 4 Cornish hens, a large roasting chicken, etc.
Sauté onions, celery and nuts in butter over medium heat until softened, about five minutes. Add remaining ingredients except for cereal and continue to cook and stir until berries burst. Remove from heat and allow to cool slightly. Stir in cereal.
Makes about 8 cups - per 1 cup: 318 calories, 26 g fat (8 g sat), 19 g carb (10 g fiber), 4 g protein

TIP: Pair my complimentary Orange-Rosemary dry rub (page 21) with Cranberry-Orange Dressing.

MUSHROOM SAGE STUFFING

1 cup butter
4 cups sliced green onions, including green tops (about 4 bunches)
2 cups celery, minced
24 oz. fresh mushrooms, washed, dried and coarsely chopped (approx. 8 cups)
1 cup walnuts, coarsely chopped (or other nuts)
1-1/2 cups plain wheat bran
1 Tb. dried marjoram
2 tsp. poultry seasoning
2 Tb. ground or rubbed sage (or more to taste)
1 tsp. black or white pepper
2 tsp. salt
2 eggs

This recipe makes enough stuffing for a 12-16 pound turkey and can be easily cut in half for a smaller yield.

Sauté celery and nuts in butter over medium heat until softened, about five minutes. Add onions and mushrooms and continue to cook and stir for another five minutes or so. Mixture will shrink some, and veggies will release quite a bit of moisture. Add the spices and herbs, taste; adjust the seasoning to your preferences. Stir in the bran, remove from heat, and allow to set until the liquid is absorbed and it cools enough so you can add the beaten eggs without having them turn into scrambled eggs from the heat. (If you have any extra liquid remaining in the vegetables, pour it off before adding the eggs.)

Makes about 12 cups - per 1 cup: 270 calories, 24 g fat (10 g sat), 12 g carb (6 g fiber), 6 g protein

Asparagus Crème

1 lb. fresh, trimmed asparagus
2 Tb. oil
1/2 cup water (or chicken or vegetable stock)
2 cups half and half cream
2 Tb. unsalted butter
1 tsp. salt
1/2 tsp. black pepper
3 Tb. fresh tarragon or savory, or 1 Tb. dried parsley
2 Tb. white wine

Drizzle asparagus with oil, salt lightly, and roast in 425 F degree oven, turning once, until tender-crisp. Chop coarsely. Place all but 1/2 cup of the chopped asparagus, the water, and the herbs in a blender and puree completely. Set aside. Melt butter, add wine, and boil until the alcohol cooks off and the liquid reduces by about half. Add pureed vegetable mixture, reserved chopped asparagus, cream, salt, and pepper, and cook over medium heat until heated through. Do not boil.

Makes 3 cups - per 1/2 cup: 199 cal, 18 g fat (8 g sat), 6 g carb (1 g fiber), 4 g protein

RECIPE VARIATIONS

Substitute other vegetables for asparagus:
1 lb. broccoli (great with fresh thyme)
204 cal, 18 g fat (8 g sat), 6 g carb (2 g fiber), 4 g protein
1 lb. carrots (try pinch of fresh grated nutmeg, cinnamon, and celery salt)
216 cal, 18 g fat (8 g sat), 10 g carb (2 g fiber), 3 g protein
1 lb. butternut squash (Cut in half, remove seeds, roast in the skin, cut side down - puree all of it.)
213 cal, 18 g fat (8 g sat), 10 g carb, 3 g protein

Beef-and-Bean Burritos

2 pounds London broil, flank steak, or other lean cut (this is a great use for game meat)
1.25 oz. package taco seasoning mix
2 Tb. olive oil
1 cup onion, chopped
1 Tb. white vinegar
small can (4.5 oz.) chopped green chilies
15 oz. can black soy beans
10 small size whole wheat la Tortillas™
2 cups (8 oz.) shredded cheese
2 tomatoes, chopped and seeded
1 cup sour cream
Fresh cilantro, chopped avocado and/or salsa for garnish - *optional items not included in analysis.*

Trim any excess fat from meat. Combine seasoning mix and olive oil and rub into all surfaces. Place in an electric slow cooker; add onion, vinegar, and green chilies. Cover; cook on low for 9 or more hours (read this as: go to work; then come home). Remove meat from pot, reserving cooking liquid. Shred meat and return to pot with reserved cooking liquid and drained beans; stir well. Heat on high for twenty minutes to warm through, stirring occasionally.

Warm tortillas one at a time and spoon a heaping 1/3 cup of meat and bean mixture in a line on one side of the tortilla. Let the filling go all the way to one edge, and stop about one inch short of the other edge. Top that with about 2 tablespoons cheese, 2 tablespoons tomato, and 2 tablespoons of sour cream; fold the empty end of each tortilla up and over the end of the filling; then roll up long-ways. Garnish as described above.

Makes 10 - per each: 500 cal, 30 g fat (12 g sat), 21 g carb (12 g fiber), 41 g protein

RECIPE NOTES: You could always cook the meat on top of the stove or in the oven for several hours instead of in a crockpot. Leftovers can be frozen individually and then reheated in the microwave, wrapped in a damp towel, with very good results.

MAIN DISHES, CASSEROLES, & SOUPS

Beef and Broccoli Salad

Using sliced deli beef makes this one REALLY convenient! If you can, ask them to slice the beef a little thicker than typical sandwich meat. A wonderful make-ahead cold supper for hot summer evenings.

1 lb. fresh broccoli (small head)
1/3 cup vegetable oil
1 red bell pepper, seeded and cut into strips
1 cup sliced fresh mushrooms
1 Tb. minced garlic
1/4 cup white or rice wine vinegar
2 Tb. soy sauce
1 tsp. red pepper flakes
1 lb. rare roast beef, cut into strips
1 cup daikon radish, sliced and cut into very thin strips (or jicama)

Prepare broccoli by washing and then dividing into florets. Peel and slice tender portions of the stalks. Prepare the pepper, daikon, and mushrooms as described.
Heat the oil in a large skillet or wok. Add the broccoli stalks and stir fry over high heat for 1-2 minutes. Next, add the florets and continue cooking for about 3 minutes, until all are tender-crisp. Remove the broccoli from the oil with a slotted spoon and transfer to a serving bowl. Stir-fry the mushrooms next and transfer to the bowl, then do the same with the pepper. Add the garlic, vinegar, soy sauce and red pepper flakes to the empty pan; stir to combine; toss with cooked vegetables and allow to cool for a few minutes before adding the raw daikon and strips of beef. Chill for several hours before serving. Lovely when garnished with slivered almonds or toasted sesame seeds.

Makes 4 servings - per each: 406 cal, 25 g fat (5 g sat), 13 g carb (4 g fiber), 32 g protein

Breakfast Burritos

1 lb. sausage, cooked and well drained
15 oz. can black soy beans, drained
4.5 oz. can chopped green chilies
4 oz. cream cheese
2 Tb. taco seasoning mix
8 large eggs
8 "large" la Tortillas™ (burrito size)
3 Tb. Tabasco™ sauce (more or less, to taste)

Combine cooked sausage with drained beans and green chilies (use the same skillet you cooked the sausage in). Add cream cheese and taco seasoning and cook and stir until melted. Remove from pan and set aside. Scramble the eggs in the same skillet next. One at a time, microwave each tortilla for about ten seconds (making it easier to roll). Lay it out flat and place about 1/2 cup meat mixture in a line on one side of the tortilla. Let the filling go all the way to one edge, and stop about one inch short of the other edge. Top the meat with about 1/4 cup of the scrambled eggs. Sprinkle Tabasco over all, to taste. Flip the empty end of the tortilla up and over the filling, then roll the long side over the roll of filling and continue to roll until closed. Wrap individually and enjoy or freeze until needed. These reheat wonderfully in the microwave for a quick meal anytime! - wrap in a damp towel for best results.

Makes 10 - per each: 464 cal, 31 g fat (11 g sat), 27 g carb (18 g fiber!!), 26 g protein

Did you know ...

Black soy beans are full of dietary fiber, making them a carb bargain. They also provide calcium, important B vitamins, and are a good source of vitamin A, iron, phosphorus, magnesium, and zinc. I prefer Eden™ brand, and have analyzed my recipes using their nutritional information.

Buffalo Bites

2 tsp. oil
1 lb. boneless chicken pieces
1/2 cup Frank's Redhot™ or similar wing sauce
3 Tb. butter

Heat a nonstick pan with oil over medium-high heat. Chop meat into bite-size pieces (you can use any meat you desire, even fish or tofu.) Cook and stir until almost done, and crispy. Add butter to pan, followed by hot sauce. Reduce heat and continue to cook and stir until sauce has reduced and thickened and meat is done.

Makes 4 servings - per each: 246 calories, 15 g fat (6 g sat), 0 g carb, 24 g protein

Chicken Vegetable Carbonara

3 cups green beans, cooked (or canned, drained)
1/2 cup diced onion
1-1/2 lbs. boneless, skinless chicken breasts
2/3 cup water
2 tsp. instant chicken bullion
6 oz. cream cheese, cubed
2/3 cup grated Parmesan cheese
2 tsp. garlic, minced
1 cup shredded Mozzarella cheese
3 Tb. real bacon bits

Lightly grease a shallow baking pan, and preheat oven to 350 F. Arrange green beans in bottom of pan and sprinkle with onions. Pound chicken breasts slightly, to make a uniform thickness. Arrange over top of beans, overlapping if needed, and season with salt and pepper. Heat water in small saucepan, then add bullion, cream cheese, and Parmesan cheese, and stir and cook until smooth. Pour over contents of baking pan. Sprinkle bacon bits over that, and bake for about 30 minutes, until hot and bubbly. Sprinkle Mozzarella cheese over everything, then return to oven for fifteen more minutes, until chicken is cooked through and cheese is melted and starting to brown. *Makes 6 servings - per each: 410 cal, 23 g fat (12 g sat), 8 g carb (2 g fiber), 45 g protein.*

Chili Con Carne

2 lb. ground beef
1/2 cup onion, chopped
1 tsp. minced garlic (2 cloves, crushed)
4 Tb. chili powder
1 Tb. instant beef bouillon
1 tsp. paprika
1 tsp. ground oregano
1 tsp. ground cumin
1/2 tsp. cayenne pepper
1-1/2 cups water
1 can stewed tomatoes, undrained (approx. 14 oz.)
1 can tomato paste (8 oz.)
1 can black soy beans, (15 oz.) rinsed and drained
Shredded cheddar cheese, sour cream, hot peppers, and chopped chives, to garnish - *optional items not included in recipe analysis*

Brown crumbled ground beef with chopped onion; drain off and discard grease. Place in crockpot with remaining ingredients, and stir to blend well. Cover and cook on low without stirring for 8-10 hours; or on high, stirring at least hourly, for 4-5 hours.

Makes about 8 cups - per cup: 408 cal, 21.5 g fat (7 g sat), 14 g carb (5 g fiber), 39 g protein

RECIPE NOTES: This recipe can also be prepared on top of a stove or in a covered casserole in the oven. You can add or delete ingredients or spices to taste - we ALWAYS include both fresh jalapeno peppers and diced, canned green chilies in our chili. I also like to toast the spices alone in the hot pan first. (Remove the spices, then proceed with recipe as written.)

Did you know ...

Tomatoes, both fresh and canned, may play a major role in fighting disease due to their high concentration of lycopene, a powerful antioxidant. Tomatoes are also a good source of vitamins A and C.

Citrus Chicken Salad

1 lb. cooked chicken, cut into strips (about 3 cups)
1 cup green onions, sliced
2 large tomatoes, cored and chopped (about 2 cups)
4 cups Romaine lettuce or other fresh greens, torn
Juice from 1 lemon (about 3 Tb.)
1 tsp. grated lemon peel (or more to taste)
1 tsp. orange extract
3 Tb. oil
2 Tb. granular Splenda™
1 egg yolk
1/3 cup water
1/2 tsp. ground ginger
1/2 tsp. salt
1/4 tsp. garlic powder
1/4 tsp. black or red pepper
4 Tb. grated Parmesan or Romano cheese

Toss chicken, onions, tomatoes, and lettuce in a large serving bowl. Place lemon juice, peel, orange extract, oil, Splenda, egg yolk, water, ginger, salt, garlic, and pepper in blender or food processor and whirl until combined. Toss dressing over salad already in bowl, garnish with grated cheese, and serve immediately.

Makes 4 servings - per each: 308 calories, 16 g fat (3 g sat), 10 g carb (1 g fiber), 30 g protein

RECIPE NOTES: Using packaged, pre-cooked grilled chicken strips from the store can really speed up the prep time for this salad! You could also use canned chicken, other leftover meats, or even tuna or salmon. IMPORTANT: This dressing is thickened with raw egg yolk and should not be served to pregnant women, the very young, very elderly, or anyone with a compromised immune system. You can substitute 1 Tb. of ThickenThin Notstarch™ or 1 tsp. guar gum for the specified egg yolk, if desired. (I much prefer the egg yolk in this particular recipe myself, which is why I present it this way.)

Cornbread Cassoulet

2 pounds ground beef
1/2 cup chopped onion
2 cans (15 oz. each) black soy beans
2 tsp. ground cumin
1 tsp. oregano
1 tsp. garlic
1/4 cup hot sauce (such as RedHot™, or use 2 Tb. or to taste of Tabasco™)
1 cup buttermilk
4 Tb. butter, melted
3 eggs
1 tsp. baking soda
3/4 tsp. salt
7 oz. can diced green chilies
1-1/2 cups protein isolate (soy or whey)
1/2 cup coarse corn meal
2 Tb. vital wheat gluten
3 cups shredded cheese (cheddar, jack, pepper-jack, Colby, or any combo)

Brown ground beef with onion over medium heat; drain off and discard any excess grease. Add undrained beans, cumin, oregano, garlic and hot sauce; blend. Remove from heat and set aside.

Preheat oven to 350 F.

Beat eggs in a large mixing bowl. Add melted butter, buttermilk, salt, and baking soda; beat well. Sprinkle green chilies, protein powder, corn meal, and gluten over liquid ingredients; stir until smooth. Set aside.

Place reserved meat mixture in a 13x9 baking pan. Top with cheese. Pour reserved cornmeal batter over all. Bake for 25-35 minutes (less for whey, longer with soy isolate) until toothpick inserted in center comes out clean.

@ 12 small servings, each: 447 cal, 26.5 g fat (12 g sat.), 12 g carb (4 g fiber), 39 g protein

@ 8 generous servings, each: 671 cal, 40 g fat (18 g sat.), 19 g carb (7 g fiber), 58 g protein

Crispy Carnitas

2 pounds pork butt (shoulder)
1/2 cup onion, chopped
2 Tb. minced garlic (about 8 fresh cloves, crushed)
1 tsp. ground cumin
1 Tb. white vinegar
2 tsp. hot pepper sauce, such as Tabasco™ (to taste)

Place all ingredients in slow-cooker and add 1 cup water. Cook on low, covered, for 9 or more hours.
Strain off the cooking liquid, reserving what's left of the chopped onion. Shred the meat, discarding any large chunks of excess fat but leaving some, and then add it and the vegetables to a hot sauté pan. Cook and stir (uncovered) over medium heat until the shredded meat becomes brown and very crispy. There should be enough fat still in the meat after slow-cooking for it to render out during this last cooking process without the need to add additional oil to the pan, but you may need to add 3-4 table-spoons of water to the pan at the beginning to get the process going without first burning everything on. By the time the water evaporates, the oil you'll need to finish should be there *if you stick to pork butt* - don't try to make this recipe with a loin or any other lean cut, or you'll be disappointed in the results.

Use the cooked meat hot or cold, in wraps, casseroles, sandwiches, etc. I prefer mine on a low carb tortilla with chopped tomato and sour cream. When I'm feeling especially indulgent, I add a whole fresh-roasted green chili to my wrap under the pork and other condiments and add shredded cheese and fresh cilantro as well.

@ 8 servings, each (pork only): 297 cal, 18 g fat (6 g sat), 1 g carb; 30 g protein

Cream of Chicken Soup

1 tsp. butter
2 tsp. minced garlic
1/4 cup minced celery
1/2 cup minced onion
3/4 cup water
1 can chicken broth (2 cups)
1 Tb. instant chicken bullion
1 cup canned chicken, drained (or cooked chicken of any kind, chopped)
1/2 cup half and half cream
1 tsp. poultry seasoning
1 Tb. parsley
Salt and pepper to taste

Sauté onion and celery in butter in saucepan until softened. Add water, broth, and bullion and bring to a boil, stirring, Add remaining ingredients and continue to cook and stir until heated through.

Makes 4 cups - per cup: 144 cal, 6 g fat (3 g sat), 4 g carb, 18 g protein

Cream of Tomato Soup

14.5 oz. can diced stewed tomatoes
2 cups water
1/4 cup half and half cream
1/4 tsp. salt
1/2 tsp. black pepper
1/2 tsp. celery salt
1 tsp. onion powder
2 tsp. instant chicken bullion
1 Tb. granular Splenda™

Puree undrained tomatoes in a blender until smooth. Place in a saucepan with remaining ingredients and cook and stir until heated through.

Makes 4 cups - per cup: 47 cal, 2 g fat (1 g sat), 6 g carb, 1 g protein

I created these soups while sick and in search of quick and legal comfort foods.

Florentine Cheddar Strata

One of my <u>favorites</u> - try reheated leftovers for breakfast with fried egg(s) broken over the top.

24 oz. spicy sausage
2 Tb. hot pepper sauce
1 cup diced onion
1 cup diced bell pepper
4 cups shredded cheese
20 oz. frozen chopped spinach
1 cup cottage cheese
1/2 cup feta cheese
1 cup TLC bake mix
2 eggs
1/2 tsp. each: salt and black pepper
4 cups chopped cauliflower
1/2 cup bacon bits
1/4 cup grated Parmesan cheese

If using link sausage, remove casings and discard. Spinach should be thawed, but not drained. Crumble sausage in pan over medium heat, and cook through, stirring occasionally. Meanwhile, chop the onion and the red pepper and clean the cauliflower. Drain all excess grease from sausage, and add chopped onion and red pepper and pepper sauce to the pan. Continue to cook, stirring, until vegetables are tender-crisp. Cook cauliflower separately and drain completely (great dish for leftovers). Chop into fine pieces and set aside. Combine spinach with cottage cheese, feta cheese, eggs, bake mix, salt, and pepper in a food processor or blender, and puree. *You may need to do this in two batches, depending on the size of your machine. Layer half of the cooked sausage mixture in 13 by 9 inch pan, then half of the shredded cheese, then all of the spinach mixture, and finally the remaining sausage and cheese. Cover this with all of the cauliflower, and press it all down firmly with the back of a spatula or your hand. Sprinkle with bacon bits and Parmesan cheese, and bake for one hour at 350 F. Allow casserole to stand for 10 minutes before serving. (Freezes & reheats well.)

16 servings - per each: 381 cal, 27 g fat (12 sat), 8 g carb (2 g fiber), 25 g protein

Four Cheese Lasagna

2 small zucchini, sliced lengthwise
1 egg
1 cup grated Parmesan cheese, divided
1/4 cup TLC bake mix
1 lb. hot sausage or ground beef
3/4 cup cottage cheese
1 cup crumbled feta cheese
1 egg
1 tsp. garlic
1-1/2 tsp. Italian Seasoning
1 Tb. parsley
1/4 cup heavy cream
4 oz. jar diced pimento, drained
1/2 cup sliced fresh mushrooms
1 tomato, in 6 slices
2 cups shredded mozzarella cheese

Grease a small oblong baking pan (11x7) and pre-heat oven to 350 F. Mix 2/3 cup of the Parmesan cheese with the bake mix and egg. With wet fingers, press this mixture into bottom of pan.

Slice the zucchini into 4 long, thick slices each, and press them down into the surface of the crust, over-lapping and trimming slightly if needed. Bake for 25-30 minutes until visible crust is deep golden brown and zucchini has begun to brown. While crust is bak-ing, crumble and cook ground meat. Top the hot squash with a layer of half of the meat.

In previously used mixing bowl, blend cottage cheese, feta, remaining 1/3 cup Parmesan cheese, egg, garlic, parsley, Italian seasoning, pimento, mushrooms, and cream. Spread this mixture over the layers already in the pan; top with remaining meat.

Bake for 30 minutes. Remove from oven, sprinkle with salt and pepper, arrange the sliced tomatoes over all, and cover with the shredded mozzarella. Bake for 15-20 more minutes, until bubbly and golden brown on top. Let stand for ten minutes at room temperature before cutting and serving.

Makes 6 servings - per each: 506 cal, 39 g fat (17 g sat), 7 g carb (1 g fiber), 27 g protein

Glazed Thai Strips

2 lb. boneless, skinless chicken breast (also good with pork and tofu)
salt and pepper
4 Tb. soy sauce
2 Tb. creamy style unsweetened peanut butter
2 Tb. oil
2 Tb. Splenda™ granular
1 tsp. ground ginger

Slice chicken into strips. Mix marinade, add meat, and allow to marinate while coming to room temperature, twenty to thirty minutes. Line a large, shallow pan with greased aluminum foil, and broil the marinated meat strips close to heat source, turning once, until meat is cooked through (approximately 4-6 minutes per side, depending on thickness). *Makes 4 servings - per each: 323 cal, 11 g fat (2 g sat), 2 g carb, 51 g protein*

RECIPE NOTE: Great cooked on a grill as kabobs, too!

Humble Crumble

1 lb. ground beef (anything works here, including cooked leftovers)
1/3 cup chopped onion
2 tsp. Italian seasoning (try substituting 2-3 Tb. of any fresh herb you like)
1/2 tsp. garlic
1/2 tsp. salt
1/4 tsp. black pepper
1/2 cup crumbled feta
1/2 cup cottage cheese
2 cups chopped spinach (may substitute other fresh greens or any leftover vegetables you have on hand)

Sauté onions with meat until done. Drain any excess grease. Add seasonings and cheeses and cook, stirring constantly, until sauce is smooth. Add greens and/or leftover veggies/meats, and stir and cook until wilted and heated through. Serve immediately. *Makes 4 servings - per each: 423 cal, 27 g fat (11 g sat), 3 g carb (1 g fiber), 38 g protein*

Italian Cheese Loaf

2 pounds ground chicken (or pork, etc.)
1 cup ricotta cheese (I like to mix ricotta and feta when making this dish with pork)
2/3 cup grated Parmesan cheese
2 eggs
2 Tb. Italian seasoning
2 tsp. minced garlic
3 Tb. dry parsley (or 1/3 cup fresh, minced)
2 Tb. red wine vinegar
1 Tb. granular Splenda™
2 Tb. olive oil
1 tsp. salt
1/2 tsp. pepper

Use your hands or a mixer on slow speed to blend all ingredients thoroughly without over-mixing.

Line a round cake pan with foil and grease it lightly. Press loaf mixture firmly into pan, and bake for 45 minutes at 350 degrees F. Drain the accumulated grease out of the pan carefully, then place another piece of foil, followed by a flat baking sheet, upside-down over the round pan with the meat in it. Flip the whole thing over, so the meat ends up on the baking sheet. Remove the round pan and carefully peel off and discard the top layer of foil.
Place under broiler until sides and top are golden and crunchy, 8-15 minutes.

Makes 8 servings - per each: 327 calories, 15 g fat (5 g sat), 2 g carb, 43 g protein

TIP: Never over-mix any meatloaf or meatball mixture - doing so can make it dry and tough (mealy).

Japanese Daikon Noodle Soup

1 tsp. olive oil
1 cup red bell pepper, cut into thin strips
1/4 cup carrot, cut into matchstick strips
2 green onions, thinly sliced (about 3 Tb.)
4 cups beef broth or prepared bullion
1 cup water
2 tsp. soy sauce
1 tsp. fresh grated ginger root (or 1/2 tsp. ground)
1/2 tsp. black or white ground pepper
1 cup thinly sliced shitake mushroom caps
1-1/2 cups prepared daikon (peeled and sliced into thin noodle-shaped strips)
1 lb. cooked, chopped chicken, pork, or firm raw tofu, drained and cubed

Heat oil in a large skillet or soup pot over medium-high heat. Add bell pepper, carrot, and onion and cook for about 3 minutes to soften vegetables slightly. Stir in broth, water, soy sauce, ginger and black pepper. Bring to a boil. Add mushrooms, daikon, and meat or tofu. Reduce heat and simmer gently for 5 minutes or until heated through. Note: You can reduce the carbs in this dish by 3 g per serving simply by omitting the shitake mushroom.

Makes 6 cups - per 1 cup: 134 cal, 3.5 g fat (0 sat), 9 g carb (1 g fiber), 18 g protein

Did you know...

The word daikon means "great root" in Japanese. Daikons are also known as Japanese radish, Oriental radish, Lo Pak, and loh baak. Daikon may be eaten raw, cooked, or preserved, and it can be substituted successfully in any almost recipe that calls for turnips. Daikons look like huge, fat, white carrots and are thought to aid in the digestion of fatty foods, being a good source of potassium, vitamin C, and folate, as well as dietary fiber.

Layered Rellanos & Southwestern Sauce

27 oz. can roasted canned green chilies
3 cups shredded cheese (any type you like)
8 large eggs
1 cup heavy cream
2 cups bacon bits, cooked chunks of meat, black soy beans, or any combination of these
1/3 cup dried onion flakes or 2/3 cup chopped fresh
14 oz. can diced tomatoes and green chilies, drained
Salt and pepper to taste

Preheat oven to 350 F. Lightly grease a 13x9 pan.

Open each pepper, removing excess seeds, skin and juice, then cover bottom of pan as evenly as possible with half of the cleaned peppers. Sprinkle with one cup of the meat and/or bean mixture, then half the onion flakes, and one cup of the cheese. Add another layer of the remaining peppers, then the remaining meat, onions, and cheese. Beat the eggs very well, then add the cream and the drained can of tomatoes and green chilies. Pour this carefully over the layers in the pan, then add black pepper to taste and bake about 50 minutes, until center is set. Allow to rest for five minutes at room temp. before serving with a dollop of my Southwestern Sauce.

@ *12 small servings, each: 506 cal, 33 g fat (19 g sat,), 9 g carb (1 g fiber), 35 g protein*
@ *8 generous servings, each: 766 cal, 49 g fat (29 g sat.), 13 g carb (2 g fiber), 53 g protein*

SOUTHWESTERN SAUCE

1 cup sour cream
4 Tb. finely minced, fresh cilantro
1 tsp. lime juice
1 tsp. granular Splenda™
1/2 tsp. cumin
1/2 tsp. oregano
1 tsp. black pepper
1 tsp. paprika
1 tsp. (more to taste?) hot pepper sauce

Makes 1 cup - per 2 Tb: 63 calories, 6 g fat (3 g sat.), 1 g carb

Maxed Out Cheddar Soup

1 lb. ground beef
1/2 cup chopped onion
4 oz. can green chilies
4 oz. cream cheese
6 cups water
1/2 cup Hormel™ bagged real bacon bits
3 cups chopped cauliflower (12 oz. raw)
1 Tb. cheddar cheese powder (optional)
1 tsp. salt
1/2 tsp. black pepper or hot pepper sauce to taste

Brown meat with onion; drain off and discard any excess grease. (I press it in a mesh colander with paper toweling, to remove as much grease as possible.) Stir in undrained green chilies and cubed cream cheese. Cook and stir until smooth. Add water, followed by remaining ingredients, and cook and stir until cauliflower is softened. Taste and adjust seasonings as needed.

Makes about 8 cups after evaporation - per 1 cup: 342 cal, 26 g fat (12 g sat), 4 g carb (1 g fiber), 17 g protein

VARIATIONS: Adding a tablespoon of chopped red pimento or fresh bell pepper looks lovely in this soup. You may substitute sausage or poultry for the beef, or use a mixture. Black beans are a great addition. You can add shredded extra sharp cheese to taste in place of the powdered cheese, or just leave both out altogether - it is a very rich and flavorful soup without them. You can use home-fried bacon, crumbled, in place of the Hormel, but be warned that it may add enough grease to your soup to leave a slight layer floating on top (it will taste great anyway, but appearance does count).

Meaty Mexican Lasagna

2 cups cooked meat of choice, chopped fine (cooked ground beef analyzed, but note that this is an excellent use for leftover meats of all types)
15 oz. can black soy beans, drained
10 oz. can Mexican-style stewed tomatoes
1 tsp. paprika
2 tsp. ground cumin
1/2 tsp. ground oregano
Salt and pepper to taste
Hot Pepper Sauce to taste (Tabasco, etc.)
6 small whole wheat la Tortillas™
2 cups shredded cheddar cheese
Salsa, sour cream, shredded lettuce, chopped tomatoes and/or olives and chopped avocadoes or guacamole, etc. for garnish - *optional items not included in recipe analysis*

Heat a pan on the stove until very hot. Pour in the stewed tomatoes and allow the liquid to mostly cook off before adding the meat, beans, hot sauce, and spices. Cook until heated through and thickened. Taste and adjust seasonings.
Grease an 11x7 pan and line it with tortillas (rip them to fit without overlapping).
Cover the tortillas with half the meat and half the cheese. Follow this with another layer of tortillas, then the rest of the meat, and the rest of the cheese. Bake at 375 F for about 20-25 minutes. Allow to rest at room temperature for five to ten minutes before serving.

8 servings - per each: 424 cal, 26 g fat (11 g sat), 20 g carb (13 g fiber), 33 g protein

Omelet TLC

Omelets can be deliciously decadent or simply satisfying, and they are also cheap and nutritious - one of my favorite combinations in food. No empty calories in these babies!

While there are few things as tasty or satisfying as a really good omelet, there are also few things as dissatisfying as a too-brown, tough, and rubbery omelet. I have yet to find a really good How-To for omelets, so this is my attempt to provide one. I'm going to describe my own method, which I arrived at only after years of trial-and-error and results that varied wildly. Now, I am aware that my methods differ from "traditional" methods and you may have very different views on this subject. If you're convinced that the "right" way to make an omelet differs from mine, then you don't need my little tutorial ... but I have had far too many people tell me over the years how they "love eating omelets in restaurants, but just can't make one at home that is any good" not to make this effort.

The most important thing you will need is a good quality, ten-inch nonstick pan. Everyone should have one of these, and they should always be replaced at the very first sign of wear or flaking. You will need some oil and eggs, most likely some cheese, and whatever else you'd like to throw in your omelet. This is a wonderful way to use up whatever leftovers you have on hand, or to create a meal from almost nothing. The most important thing I can tell you about making a good omelet is this: Haste does make waste! It is crucial to not get the pan too hot. Don't be in a hurry. Even taking your time, you can cook an omelet in less than 15 minutes. Never turn the heat to above the medium setting, even when doing the initial heating of the pan. Depending on your stove, you may not want to turn the burner setting above medium-low at any point in this process.

First, allow the pan to heat up for about 3 or 4 minutes over medium heat with nothing in it.

While the pan is heating, beat three eggs very well and chop your pre-cooked fillings, grate the cheese, etc... I like to use a blender to whip the eggs. Do not add any additional liquid to the eggs. Doing so simply increases the likelihood that you will tear your omelet. Pour 1-2 tablespoons of a good oil into the preheated pan, followed immediately by the well-beaten eggs. Sprinkle the eggs with salt and pepper to taste. This next instruction may be the hardest one for most people: Don't do another thing for several minutes! Just let the eggs start to set up without messing with them. When the eggs have begun to set up well, which you will be able to see because the sides will start to shrink away from the pan, lower the heat a little more, to medium-low.

Once you can take the spatula and tease up the sides of the omelet and see that it is holding together fairly well on the bottom (which should not be browned at all at this point) then you may hold the spatula at a 90 degree angle to the pan (handle pointing at the ceiling) and gently lift and push the sides of the omelet towards the middle, picking the pan up and tilting it as you do so, allowing the more liquid eggs on the top to run underneath the already-set part. Don't do this too vigorously, because as long as the heat under the pan is not too high, you will be able to cook the eggs through without browning or burning them. This lift and tilt method just speeds the whole process up.

When the eggs are almost cooked through and there is very little liquid that can be seen on the top, stack the desired fillings all on one half of the pan. Slide your spatula under the empty side, and gently flip that over the filling, closing the omelet. Allow the omelet to sit in the pan over the low heat and continue to cook for another two to three minutes, to complete cooking through and allow any cheese to melt. Do not use a lid to cover the omelet pan at any point. Doing so will steam the eggs and make them tough.

Use your imagination when it comes to satisfying combinations of fillings. One of my favorites when is lump crabmeat, fresh chopped parsley or cilantro, thinly sliced very ripe avocado, crisp bacon, and cream cheese. Picture that, then imagine smothering it with the quick and easy blender hollandaise sauce recipe from page 21. How about leftover taco meat, black olives, and shredded pepper jack, topped with sour cream and salsa or guacamole? When I have leftover steak in the house, I slice it and sauté it in a little oil and Worcestershire sauce with some onions and pepper strips and make myself a "Philly cheese steak" omelet. Omelets can also be delicious when their contents are as simple as some finely diced onion and a slice of whatever cheese you have around, including American. You can even add a little sweetener to your eggs, then fill an omelet with a mixture of cream cheese, cottage cheese, or ricotta, along with some chopped fresh fruit. Top this with some yogurt and/or a drizzle of SF syrup for a meal that is definitely out of the ordinary!

Here are some common combinations and the nutritional analysis for each. Half of one is often enough for me, especially when paired with a salad.

DENVER OMELET
2 tsp. butter
1/4 cup each: chopped onion and diced bell pepper, sautéed in the butter
3 eggs
3 slices deli ham, diced
1/2 cup shredded Colby-Jack or other cheese
632 cal, 44 g fat (21 g sat), 8 g carb (1 g fiber), 48 g protein

TACO OMELET
3 eggs
1/2 cup shredded cheese
1/2 cup taco-seasoned ground beef
2 Tb. each sour cream and salsa, for garnish (included in this analysis)
635 cal, 47 g fat (22 sat), 8 g carb (1 g fiber), 42 g protein

PLAIN CHEESE
3 eggs
1/2 cup shredded cheddar
465 cal, 35 g fat (16 g sat), 3 g carb, 32 g protein

Perfect Prime Rib

Prime Rib roast, any size
Salt
Garlic Powder
Freshly ground black pepper, to taste

Preheat oven to 425 degrees F. Season roast with moderate amounts of salt, garlic, and pepper, rubbing well into entire outside surface of roast with your hands. Place roast, fat side up, on rack in a roasting pan. (A roast with intact rib bones can be placed in such a way that the ribs themselves act as a rack, and you can skip the rack in that case. You may also ask your butcher to, or you can, remove the bones yourself, for easier serving later - I find the final taste unaffected, although purists would argue that the bones impart flavor and shouldn't be removed before roasting.)

Roast for 30 minutes; reduce heat to 350 degrees F and continue to cook at that temperature until a meat thermometer inserted deep into the meat registers the desired doneness (an hour to two more, depending on size of roast). Large roasts continue to cook for several minutes after being removed from the oven, while resting, so you should remove them when within five degrees of the desired serving temperature, and not wait until they actually reach that point. For beef roasts, 140 F = rare, 150 F = medium, and 160 F = well done. For "medium to medium well" - pink in the middle, but not red, remove beef roast from the oven when a meat thermometer registers 145-150 in the very center. Because the smaller end pieces will always be more done than the larger ones in the center, unless you overcook the entire roast, there should be a variety available when serving. Transfer roast to a carving platter and let rest, covered loosely with foil, for 10-20 minutes before carving. I like to remove the bones first, then slice the roast into manageable servings, since merely cutting between the bones can yield servings that are thicker than necessary for an average diner. The only carbs here come from the garlic powder and are usually negligible.

TRADITIONAL AU JUS

2 cups beef stock, canned broth, or prepared bullion
1/2-1 teaspoon dried thyme, to taste
1 Tb. or more Worcestershire sauce, to taste
Salt and freshly ground pepper, to taste
Remove excess fat from surface of pan drippings and discard. Add beef stock and thyme. Bring to a boil and simmer, stirring, for 10 minutes. Season with Worcestershire and salt and pepper to taste. Transfer to a serving dish and pass with sliced beef.
Again, the only carbs here come from the Worcestershire and are greatly diluted when divided among the many servings yielded, making them negligible.

Pizza TLC

TLC CRUST:
About 2/3 cup warm water (start with 1/2 cup and add more, 1 Tb. at a time, only if needed)
2 Tb. olive oil
1 cup grated Parmesan cheese
1/2 cup whole grain wheat flour (or oat flour)
2 Tb. vital wheat gluten
3 Tb. dry milk powder (or plain whey powder)
1 pkg. dry yeast (reduce by 1/2 tsp. @ high altitude)
Place water and oil in bread machine. Lightly mix together the Parmesan, flour, gluten, and milk powder. Pour mixture in machine over liquid (do not mix). Make a well in the top of the dry ingredients and place the yeast in the well. Process on dough setting. Keep an eye on it during mixing, and add more water if necessary. Spread risen dough out in a greased, large pizza pan and bake in a preheated 375 F oven for ten minutes. Remove from oven (may have an air bubble, just push it flat if so). Add additional toppings as desired, then return to oven until done.
Per batch: 1049 cal, 70 g fat (25 g sat), 60 g carb (6 g fiber), 64 g protein

RECIPE NOTES: I enjoy this crust plain as a rustic dipping cracker, paired with Garlic Schmear (pg. 28). You can also mix this by hand instead of in a bread machine - see Yeast Bread TLC on page 124 for guidelines.

BUFFALO CHICKEN PIZZA

1 prepared crust (pg. 69)
4 oz. softened cream cheese
1/3 cup Ranch dressing
13 oz. can chicken, drained (or 2 cups cubed, cooked leftover chicken)
1/2 cup Redhot™ wing sauce
1 cup shredded mozzarella cheese

Prepare crust as directed. Mix cream cheese and ranch dressing together and spread over partially baked crust. Drain chicken and toss with hot sauce. Scatter pieces over white sauce. Top with mozzarella and return to oven for another 20 minutes or so.

8 slices - per each: 291 cal, 19 g fat (7 g sat), 7 g carb, 23 g protein

VARIATION: Chop two or three fresh jalapeno or serano peppers or half a bell pepper and scatter over white sauce along with meat.

SUPREME PIZZA

1 crust, prepared
1/4 cup tomato paste + 1/3 cup warm water
2 tsp. Italian seasoning
1/2 tsp. garlic powder
1/4 tsp. black pepper
2 oz. sliced pepperoni
1 Tb. real bacon bits
2 Tb. minced onion
2 Tb. minced bell pepper
1 Tb. chopped black olives
1/2 cup sliced fresh mushrooms
3 cups shredded mozzarella cheese

Prepare crust as directed. Mix tomato paste and water with spices and spread over partially baked crust. Arrange pepperoni, bacon, and vegetable pieces over sauce. Top with mozzarella and return to oven for another 20 minutes or so.

8 slices - per each: 279 cal, 18 g fat (8 g sat), 12 g carb (2 g fiber), 21 g protein.

Quiche TLC

Quiche is easy to assemble, economical, delicious, and extremely versatile. It is "fair game" for any meal, at any time of day.

Quiche is basically just a savory custard which is baked in the shape of a pie, with various added ingredients, usually (but not always) including cheese, cooked meat, and vegetables. This makes it an ideal dish in which to use up leftovers! In fact, I often make twice as much as I need for a meat-and-veggie meal, on purpose, knowing full well that the leftovers can be efficiently transformed the next night in a quiche which will seem like an entirely different meal. "Real Women" (and men) just don't have time to reinvent the wheel every night; anytime that I can cook two meals at once, I consider myself blessed.

BASIC QUICHE

2 cups cream - any style works - nutritional counts based on half-and-half cream
4 eggs
Salt and Pepper
1 to 2 cups cooked chopped meat and/or vegetables
1 to 2 cups shredded cheese - typical "classic" quiches almost always specify Swiss cheese, but you can use anything you like. I usually prefer to use 1/2 cup grated Parmesan (the real stuff please, grated freshly off a block and not simply poured out a green can) and 1 cup mixed, shredded other cheeses. Occasionally, I use some cream cheese or even feta, goat, cottage, bleu, or ricotta.

Scatter the chopped filling ingredients and cheeses into a well-greased pie pan, no need for any crust, and pour the well-beaten egg and cream mixture over the top. Bake at 425 F for 15 minutes, then lower the heat to 350 and bake another 30 minutes, until a knife inserted in the center comes out clean. Allow to set at room temperature for 5-10 minutes before serving. *Reduce the cream a little when using moist filling ingredients, such as canned or frozen vegetables.

I figure 8 servings per quiche - assuming (for example) you used 1-1/2 cups shredded cheddar, 1 cup chopped cooked broccoli, and 1 cup (5 oz) chopped cooked chicken while following the above guide, each serving would then equal: *240 calories, 18 g fat (9 sat), 4 g carb, 16 g protein.*

Here are several of my favorite variations on this theme; follow the same basic assembly and cooking instructions given for Basic Quiche.

GARDEN QUICHE
3/4 cup diced unpeeled zucchini
3/4 cup minced red bell pepper
1/2 cup sliced fresh mushrooms
1 Tb. grated white onion
4 oz. (1 cup) shredded extra-sharp white cheddar
4 oz. cream cheese, cubed
4 eggs
1-1/2 cups cream
8 servings - per each: 211 cal, 17 g fat (9 sat), 5 g carb, 9 g protein

FLORENTINE QUICHE
10 oz. frozen chopped spinach, drained thoroughly (about 1 cup)
1/2 cup grated Parmesan cheese
1/2 cup diced Swiss cheese
1 cup chopped cooked ham or 1/3 cup bacon bits
2 Tb. minced onion, sautéed in 1 Tb. oil or butter (or cooked along with the bacon)
4 eggs
1-1/2 cups cream
8 servings - per each: 210 cal, 15 g fat (7 sat), 4 g carb (1 g fiber), 14 g protein

MEDITERRANEAN QUICHE
1/2 cup pitted, sliced olives
3/4 cup crumbled feta or goat cheese
1 cup grated Parmesan or Provolone cheese
3 garlic cloves, finely minced
1 small Roma tomato, seeded, chopped and drained
1 cup marinated artichoke hearts, finely chopped

and well-drained
1 cup chopped cooked meat (optional but I like to use and analyzed chicken breasts)
1-1/2 cups cream
4 eggs
8 servings - per each: 228 cal, 15.5 g fat (8 sat), 5 g carb, 16 g protein

SEAFOOD QUICHE
2 cans drained lump crabmeat or tiny shrimp
4 oz. cream cheese, cubed
3/4 cup grated Parmesan cheese
3 Tb. chopped fresh dill weed
1/4 cup fresh lemon juice
2 tsp. lemon zest
2 Tb. pimento
2 cups cream
4 eggs
8 servings - per each: 236 cal, 17 g fat (9 sat), 4 g carb, 16 g protein

MEXICAN FIESTA QUICHE
15 oz. can black soy beans, drained and rinsed
1 cup taco-seasoned ground beef
1 sliced avocado
2 Tb. chopped black olives
2 cups shredded pepper jack cheese
1/3 cup chopped green chilies (or jalapenos)
2 cups cream
4 eggs
8 servings - per each: 307 cal, 23 g fat (9 sat), 7 g carb (4 g fiber), 19 g protein

Did you know ...

Eggs are an almost perfect food, containing the highest quality protein available, as well as almost every essential vitamin and mineral needed by humans (the exception being Vitamin C - because chickens produce their own and need none in their diet).

Roast Rack of Lamb

Marinating lamb twice brings out a depth of flavor unmatched by any other preparation. Serve with a medley of roasted vegetables and a fresh green salad for a simple meal that will appear to be anything but...

2 racks of lamb ribs, 1-1.5 pounds each (about 8 rib bones to each, backbone should be removed)
1/2 cup red wine (I prefer a good Merlot or Cabernet)
1/4 cup balsamic vinegar
1 Tb. granular Splenda™
3 Tb. water
1 Tb. dry onion flakes (or 1/4 cup minced, fresh)
1 tsp. ground dry thyme (or 1 Tb. chopped, fresh)
1/2 tsp. black pepper (freshly ground, please)

Trim and discard as much excess fat from the racks of lamb as you can, to within 1/4 inch or less. Mix the remaining ingredients in a deep dish suitable for marinating. Add the lamb and turn to coat all sides well. Place in the refrigerator, covered, for at least one hour and for as many as six hours. Remove lamb from marinade and allow excess liquid to drip off, while you preheat a non-stick fry pan over medium-high heat. (Reserve the remaining marinade!)

Sear all sides of the lamb racks well, then return them to the marinade, cover, and chill again, for 1-4 hours.

Place lamb in a shallow roasting pan, bone side down (it is okay if the bones overlap; arrange the meat portions so that their sides do not touch, if possible.) Pour the marinade over the top and roast in a hot 450 F oven until the racks test done with a meat thermometer, inserted into the center of each meat portion, not touching bones. (If all of the marinade evaporates before the lamb tests done, add small amounts of water as needed to prevent scorching.) You may remove lamb from the oven when the center registers 125 F for rare - this will only take about half an hour, depending on the size of the racks. Medium rare = 135 degrees, and well done, which "they" say you shouldn't do, occurs at just

145 degrees. Allow the racks to rest at room temperature for at least 5 minutes before dividing them into 2 portions each and serving, during which time the internal temperature of the meat will go up another 5 degrees or so.

Makes 4 servings - per each: 690 cal, 37 g fat (13 g sat), 4 g carb, 74 g protein

---

Did you know ...

All oils are not created equal. Some oils have an unstable molecular structures, and can become actively harmful if heated and then consumed. Guidelines for use of some common oils:

WORST - DO NOT CONSUMER UNDER ANY CONDITIONS: Margarine or anything hydrogenated (some add canola, a.k.a rapeseed, to this list)

BEST FOR **COLD USE ONLY**: Flax, Evening Primrose, Walnut, Peanut, Light Sesame

BEST FOR **COOKING OR COLD USE**: Grapeseed, Macadamia, Coconut, Palm, Olive, Butter, Clarified Butter (Ghee), and Lard (use lard only when made without any hydrogenated additives)

Store oils carefully, out of light and in a cool, dry place like the refrigerator. If oil tastes bitter to you, throw it away, as it has probably spoiled. Don't buy refined oils. (They will say "refined" on the label.) Look for cold-pressed or expeller-pressed oil, which means the oil is expressed at lower temperatures, which is thought to be better for you.

Unrefined palm and coconut oils are semi-solid at room temperatures and make an excellent substitute for shortening.

Savory Breakfast Bites

2 pounds spicy sausage
3/4 cup chopped onion
1/2 cup diced bell pepper
3 cups sharp cheddar cheese, shredded
6 eggs
2 cups TLC bake mix
1 cup half-and-half cream
1 cup whole milk plain yogurt (or sour cream, or cottage cheese)
1 tablespoon onion powder
1 tablespoon garlic powder
2 Tb. hot pepper sauce (such as Tabasco™)
Salt and black pepper to taste

Preheat oven to 350 F. Crumble and cook the sausage with the onions and peppers; drain grease. Set aside to cool.

Mix the shredded cheese and cooled sausage together.

In a separate bowl, preferably with a poor spout, blend the eggs, cream, yogurt, and spices with the bake mix and hot sauce.

Put a small amount of the meat & cheese mixture in the bottom of each of 24 lined or very well-oiled muffin tins. I like to use a small oiled cookie scoop to do this. Next, pour the batter out evenly over the meat and cheese. Finally, top off the batter in each tin with the remaining meat and cheese mixture, (let it sit on top, do not mix it in or poke it down).

Bake for 20 to 30 minutes, until golden brown. Run a sharp knife around the edge of each muffin tin and immediately remove to paper plates to drain and cool.

Makes 24 muffins - per each: 267 cal, 19 g fat (8 g sat), 5 g carb, 17 g protein

VARIATIONS: Add chopped, cooked vegetables, or vary or omit the meats. Add a small amount of salsa to the egg batter for some extra kick.

Sour Cream Chicken Enchiladas

2 cups (24 oz.) cooked, chopped chicken
1 cup sour cream
1 Tb. ThickenThin Notstarch™ or 1 tsp. guar gum
1 Tb. hot pepper sauce
1/4 cup half and half cream
1 cup water (or broth from canned chicken)
7 oz. can diced green chilies (or 3/4 cup diced, fresh-roasted chili peppers)
4 oz. jar pimentos (or 1/3 cup diced, fresh-roasted red pepper)
3 Tb. minced fresh cilantro leaves (or more to taste)
2 cups shredded cheese
6 small whole wheat la Tortillas™

Preheat oven to 350 F. Drain chicken if using canned, reserve liquid; set both aside. Stir starch into the sour cream until smooth, then stir in hot sauce and cream until blended, then slowly add water. Pour enough of the resulting sauce into a 7x11 pan to cover the bottom, and set aside. Open a wrap and arrange about 1/3 cup chicken in a line down the center. Sprinkle with 1/2 Tb. cilantro, and 1 tsp. each of pimento and diced green chili, then 1/3 cup cheese. Roll up as tightly as you can, then place it, seam side down, in the prepared pan. Continue on in this manner until all 6 shells are rolled. Add all but 1 tsp. of the remaining pimento and green chilies to the reserved sauce, then pour it evenly over the enchiladas. Sprinkle the top with the last few diced peppers and any remaining cilantro. Cover tightly with foil and bake for 50 minutes; uncover and continue to bake for an additional ten minutes, until golden brown on edges and heated through.

Makes 6 servings - per each: 470 cal, 29 g fat (15 g sat), 22 g carb (10 g fiber), 41 g protein

Spicy Goulash

6 oz. spicy sausage (bulk, crumbled or 3 large links, removed from casing and sliced - I prefer chorizo)
1/3 cup chopped onion
2 tsp. minced garlic
1 tsp. ground oregano (or 1 Tb. fresh, which is highly recommended)
1 tsp. marjoram
1 small, fresh jalapeno or serrano pepper, sliced (remove seeds if you don't like lots of spice)
3 oz. fresh or canned mild green chilies, chopped
2 cans diced tomatoes (14.5 oz. each)
2 cups diced zucchini or yellow squash
1-1/2 cups shredded mozzarella cheese

In a large fry pan, cook sausage and onion. Drain any excess if there is a lot of grease, but if there's just a little, leave it. Add garlic and herbs and cook for one to two minutes more, then add tomatoes and diced squash and continue to cook for about ten minutes, while sauce reduces and squash becomes tender-crisp.

Place goulash in a large, shallow pan, spread the mozzarella over the top, and place under broiler until bubbly and golden. (If your fry pan handle is oven-proof, you will not need to dirty a separate pan for this step.)

Makes 6 servings - per each: 256 cal, 16 g fat (7 g sat), 11 g carb (1 g fiber), 16 g protein

Did you know ...

Capsaicin, the active agent that provides the heat and spice in chili peppers, has been shown to produce a myriad of health benefits and is being studied as an anti-inflammatory and pain relief agent, as well as a treatment for blood clotting disorders.

Capsaicin even appears to increase metabolic rate (it could make you burn more calories).

Spicy Sausage Jambalaya

6 oz. spicy sausage (bulk, crumbled or 3 large links, removed from casing and sliced)
1 cup diced onion
1/2 cup chopped celery
2 tsp. minced garlic
1 Tb. each: onion powder, black pepper, paprika
1 tsp. salt or seasoned salt
4 oz. can diced jalapenos, drained
14 oz. can stewed tomatoes, undrained
1 cup water (those who can afford some extra carbs should use 28 oz. of tomatoes and omit this water)
5 cups grated fresh cauliflower, lightly packed (625 g, one small head or half a large head)
1 cup shredded mozzarella cheese (optional)

Fry the sausage in a large, oven-proof skillet over medium heat until sausage is browned and vegetables are soft. Add garlic and spices and cook and stir for two more minutes. Add jalapenos, tomatoes, and cauliflower and simmer and stir uncovered, for twenty to thirty minutes, stirring occasionally, until liquid is reduced and thickened and cauliflower is cooked through. Sprinkle with mozzarella and place under broiler until cheese is melted, bubbly, and browning.

Makes 6 servings - per each: 305 cal, 21 g fat (7 sat), 14 g carb (4 g fiber), 22 g protein

VARIATION: Add any type of cooked, chopped meat in addition to or in place of the sausage. Fresh peeled shrimp is a delicious and classic addition to jambalaya and adds no carbs to speak of. Add it during the last ten minutes of cooking.

Stir-Fried Beef & Broccoli

16 oz. lean flank steak, sliced thinly
2 Tb. soy sauce
2 Tb. Worcestershire sauce
2 tsp. minced garlic
2 tsp. hot pepper sauce (such as Tabasco™)
2 Tb. oil
1/2 cup onion, vertically sliced (julienned)
16 oz. mixed broccoli and cauliflower florets
1 small can water chestnuts, drained (or 1 cup thinly sliced daikon radish)

The day or morning before, slice the beef thinly (or ask the store to do it when you buy it!) Tip: Meat slices more easily and thinly when partially frozen. Mix the soy sauce with the Worcestershire, garlic, and the pepper sauce, and place it all in a large plastic bag. Add the thinly sliced meat, mix to coat evenly, remove excess air from the bag, seal tightly, and refrigerate for 6 to 24 hours.

Twenty minutes before serving, add the oil to a very hot large pan or wok, followed by the prepared vegetables. Sauté just until the largest florets are tender, but are still fairly crisp. Remove the vegetables to a covered dish to stay warm. Start adding strips of meat to the very hot pan, slowly. Leave space between each strip - DO NOT add too much of the meat all at once, or instead of browning the meat will just release the marinade trapped inside and sit there boiling in it. The strips should brown nicely and cook in just a couple of minutes each. Take care to brown each side, removing strips to the covered dish as needed, until all are cooked. Add the reserved cooked vegetables/strips and any leftover marinade back to pan and continue to cook and stir for 3-4 more minutes, until the marinade has boiled sufficiently for safety, and also has reduced to almost nothing. You may need to add a couple tablespoons of water to the pan at this point to make a sauce, if there is not enough additional liquid available already. *Makes 4 servings - per each: 387 cal, 22 g fat (7 g sat), 9 g carb (3 g fiber), 36 g protein*

Sweet & Sour Anything

2 lbs. skinless, boneless chicken breast (you can successfully use cooked or raw pork, turkey, beef, tofu, fish, shellfish, etc. - but I had to choose just one for analysis, and this is it)
salt and pepper
3 Tb. oil
1 cup red bell pepper, julienned
1 cup green bell pepper, julienned
1/2 onion, in large pieces
2 Tb. unsalted butter
1/3 cup cherry flavored SF syrup
1/4 cup pineapple flavor SF syrup
1/4 cup diet cola (non-aspartame sweetened, such as Diet Rite™)
1 tsp. ground ginger
1/8 tsp. ground cinnamon

Cut meat into bite-size pieces and season each piece with salt and pepper. Heat oil in a large skillet over medium-high heat. Add meat in small batches, slowly, so as to not crowd pan. Set cooked pieces aside once browned and cooked through; keep warm. (Skip this step when using fish, shellfish, or already cooked protein sources.)
Add butter, onions, and peppers to skillet; cook just until veggies are tender-crisp. Reduce heat to medium. Stir in syrups, cola, ginger, and cinnamon. Add previously cooked protein sources to pan and simmer gently, uncovered, stirring occasionally, until liquid is reduced and thickened to desired consistency, about twenty minutes.

NOTE: When using raw fish or shellfish or other ingredients that cook quickly in liquid and should not be overcooked, add for last ten minutes of cooking only, after the liquids have already reduced for at least ten minutes.

Makes 4 generous servings - per each: 431 cal, 24 fat (6 g sat), 7 g carb (1 g fiber), 49 g protein

Sweet & Spicy Pork & Peppers

2 lb. lean, boneless pork or chicken, cut into serving size pieces (you can actually use any protein source you want, including shrimp or tofu)
salt and pepper
1 Tb. oil
1 Tb. unsalted butter
1 large red or green bell pepper, julienned
3/4 - 1 tsp. pineapple extract/flavoring (must adjust for differences in taste and between brands)
1/2 cup white wine
1 tsp. ground ginger (or 1-2 Tb. fresh grated ginger root)
1/4 cup granular Splenda™
1-2 Tb. fresh or canned jalapeno, habanera or chili pepper, minced (optional)
1/8 tsp. ground cinnamon
3 Tb. salsa or Picante sauce

Season each piece of meat lightly with salt and pepper. Heat the oil in a large skillet over medium heat. Add meat; turn and cook until tender and cooked through. Set aside; keep warm.
Add butter and red bell pepper to same skillet; cook just until pepper is crisp-tender. Reduce heat to medium-low. Stir in pineapple extract, wine, ginger, pepper, sweetener, and cinnamon; add cooked meat pieces back to the pan and simmer all, uncovered, until liquid reduces as desired.

Makes 4 generous servings - per each: 558 cal, 25 g fat (9 g sat), 6 g carb (1 g fiber), 68 g protein

Tortilla Soup with Black Beans

4 cups canned chicken broth (2 cans)
1 Tb. fresh or bottled lime juice
4 oz. can diced green chilies
2 tsp. minced garlic
16 oz. can black soy beans, undrained
1.25 oz. pkg. taco seasoning mix
3 Tb. minced fresh cilantro
Simply combine everything in a saucepan and heat through.
Makes 4 cups - per 1 cup: 174 cal, 6 g fat (0 sat), 15 g carb (7 g fiber), 16 g protein

Tuna Cakes

24 oz. well-drained canned albacore tuna
1 tsp. salt
2 tsp. lemon juice
3/4 cup grated Parmesan cheese
2 eggs
3-4 Tb. oil for frying
1/2 tsp. paprika
Heat a large skillet over medium high heat. Sprinkle salt and lemon juice over drained tuna. Add Parmesan and broken eggs to bowl and mix lightly until blended, but do not over mix. Form into 8 even patties. Add oil to hot pan, followed a moment later by the formed patties. Sprinkle with paprika. Fry for approximately 8 minutes per side, until golden and crunchy.
Makes 4 servings - per each: 429 cal, 21 g fat (6 g sat), 1 g carb, 54 g protein

RECIPE NOTES: Regular tuna does not perform as well as albacore in this recipe. Well-drained tuna does make a difference. You can substitute cooked, flaked salmon, haddock, crab, etc., even chicken or ham - whatever leftovers or cans you have on hand. I often double this recipe since leftovers reheat well in the microwave and make terrific, quick lunches.

Velvet Soup

1 lb. chicken pieces
6 cups water
2 tablespoons dry onion flakes
1 teaspoon each: poultry seasoning, garlic powder, salt
1/2 teaspoon each: sage, celery salt, black pepper, marjoram
1 tablespoon parsley
2 tsp. instant chicken bouillon
1-1/2 cups fresh, chopped spinach (or use 1 can or small frozen bag/box, undrained)
8 ounces cream cheese, cubed
1 tablespoon hot pepper sauce
1 tablespoon soy sauce
2 teaspoons minced garlic
2 Tb. Parmesan cheese, grated
1 hard-boiled egg
1/2 tsp. paprika

Combine chicken, water, onion flakes, and dry spices including bullion. Bring to a boil, stir well, then reduce the heat to low. Simmer gently, covered, for approximately 45 minutes. Remove cooked meat from the pan, and set aside to cool slightly.

Pour remaining contents of sauce pan into a blender, add spinach, minced garlic, cream cheese, pepper sauce, and soy sauce. (You may need to do this in two batches, depending on the size of your blender. If you have an immersible wand blender, use it.)

Puree soup and return to sauce pan. Chop chicken into bite-size pieces, discarding any skin or bones, return to sauce pan, heat through, then serve.

Sprinkle each serving with a some grated Parmesan, finely chopped hard-boiled egg, and a dash of paprika for color.

Makes 8 cups - per 2 cups: 400 cal, 26 g fat (14 g sat), 9 g carb (2 g fiber), 33 g protein

All Purpose TLC Bake Mix

3 cups golden flax meal (can use brown, too)
2-1/2 cups soy protein isolate (or wheat protein isolate - but I do prefer the texture of soy best, myself)
2 cups unflavored whey protein powder
2 cups stone-ground whole wheat flour
1 cup vital wheat gluten
1/2 cup powdered whole egg
5 Tb. baking powder (reduce to 4 Tb. @ high altitude)
4 tsp. baking soda
2 tsp. salt
Mix ingredients well and use wherever bake mix is specified. Store this mix refrigerated.
I have eliminated nut meal from this version in favor of flax meal, but you can use the two interchangeably if you prefer nut meal to flax meal.

Makes 11 cups - 1 per cup: 389 cal, 11 g fat (0 sat), 32 g carb (11 g fiber), 45 g protein

Did you know ...

Flax seeds are high in antioxidants and dietary fiber, as well as lignans, which have anti-tumor properties. Flax is the most concentrated known food source of alpha-linolenic acid (ALA), the plant form of omega 3 fatty acids, which have been shown to lower high blood cholesterol and triglyceride levels as well as high blood pressure, the insulin requirement of diabetics, and allergic responses. Omega 3s may help inflammatory conditions with diseases ending in "itis".

Add ground seeds (meal) to yogurt, baked goods, casseroles, and cereals. Sprinkle seeds over vegetable dishes, salads, etc.

Apple Cheese Torte

12 oz. cream cheese, softened and divided
4 oz. butter, softened
1-1/4 cups TLC Bake mix
1-1/2 cups granular Splenda™, divided
2 Tb. SF vanilla syrup
1/2 cup plain yogurt
2 eggs
4 cups thinly sliced zucchini (4 small squash or 2 medium, to imitate green apples - do not peel; split long ways first, then slice, to shape like half moons)
2 tsp. ground cinnamon
1/2 tsp. ground nutmeg
1/2-1 tsp. apple flavoring or extract - must adjust for differences between brands
1 Tb. ThickenThin Notstarch™ or 1 tsp. guar gum
1/2 cup sliced almonds or chopped walnuts

Preheat oven to 350 F. Cream 4 oz. of the cream cheese with the butter. Cut in the bake mix and 1/2 cup of the Splenda until mixture resembles large crumbs. Press in the bottom of a 10 inch deep-dish spring-form pan.

Cream remaining 8 oz. cream cheese with 1/2 cup of remaining Splenda, yogurt, eggs, and vanilla syrup. Spread this over the crust in the pan.

Combine remaining 1/2 cup Splenda, cinnamon, nutmeg, and starch. Sprinkle apple extract over sliced zucchini; toss with cinnamon mixture. Layer evenly over contents of pan. Sprinkle nuts over all.

Bake for 45-55 minutes.

12 servings - per each: 270 cal, 22 g fat (11 g sat), 10 g carb (2 g fiber), 9 g protein

VARIATION: Made with 4 sliced real apples instead of the zucchini and flavoring, each serving would have: *291 cal, 22 g fat (11 g sat), 15 g carb (3 g fiber), 9 g protein.*

Bagels

MACHINE METHOD, ALL VARIETIES:
Lightly mix flours (and any nuts, fruits, or similar added ingredients). Start out by mixing just the 1 cup of oat flour with the other dry ingredients, and reserve the other half-cup - only add part or all of the other half-cup as needed. If the dough looks too wet after the first dry ingredients are incorporated, then add a little of the oat flour at a time until it looks right. (All carb counts include the highest measurement). Beat liquid ingredients with any salt and sweeteners specified. Add wet and dry ingredients and yeast to your machine in order suggested by manufacturer. Process on 'dough 'setting. Watch it mix, and add a little more water or flour as needed to form a ball.

ALTERNATE HAND METHOD, ALL VARIETIES:
In mixing bowl, combine the yeast and sweetener in warm water. (If you live in a humid climate, reduce water by 2 Tb. to start.) Make sure the water you use is only baby-bottle warm - adding yeast to water that is much over 105 F can kill yeast, which is a living organism and does have a shelf life. Let the yeast mixture stand until gets foamy, about 10 minutes. If the reconstituted yeast does not begin to foam and "grow" by the end of the ten minutes, try again with new yeast.
Combine all remaining dry ingredients, and any nuts, fruits, or similar added ingredients, and stir or whisk to blend them well. *Start out with by mixing just the 1 cup of oat flour with the other dry ingredients; reserve the other half-cup for use while kneading.
Add melted butter, eggs, and salt to yeast mixture; beat well. Slowly add the mixed dry ingredients, 1/2 cup at a time, stirring well after each addition. Use reserved remaining oat flour to "flour" your kneading surface. Turn the formed dough out onto the floured surface, and begin kneading. Knead until smooth and elastic, perhaps 10 minutes - more or less kneading may be needed, depending on technique. (Kneading with a stand mixer and dough

hook instead of by hand is encouraged.) Lightly oil the mixing bowl you used previously, place the dough back in it, then turn dough over once, so as to coat the surface lightly with oil.

While kneading, bring 2 cups of water to a full boil inside your microwave oven. Cover the bowl containing the kneaded dough with a clean, slightly damp cloth or some plastic wrap, and place it inside the microwave - just push the warm water into one corner and leave it there, where it will continue warming the area slightly while the dough rises. Leave the dough to rise inside the closed, turned off microwave until doubled in volume, roughly 40-60 minutes.

ALL METHODS: Grease two large baking sheets well, or line with parchment. Poke down into the risen dough deeply with two fingers, to deflate it, then knead it lightly two or three times to remove any remaining air. Using a sharp knife, divide dough into 18 equal portions. Use your fingers to stretch the top of each portion of dough down and over the rest, tucking the edges up into the center, forming a smooth ball of dough. Thrust your thumb through the center of this dough ball to meet your pointer finger, forming a hole. Keeping your fingers closed, twirl the dough like a hoola hoop to widen the hole you've made, and stretch the bagel. Place formed bagels on prepared baking sheet, cover with a clean cloth, and allow to rise slightly, for twenty minutes. While they rise, preheat the oven to 350 degrees F and bring a large pot of water to a full boil.

Place two or three of the rested bagels into the boiling water at a time. It will take about two minutes for them to change appearance and seem to swell and become water-logged. Fish them out of the water with a slotted utensil and allow to drain well before placing each one back on the baking sheet. Bake the boiled bagels for about 20 minutes, until golden. Cool thoroughly on a wire rack before wrapping and storing. Store cooled bagels in the refrigerator for up to a week. Freeze if longer storage is required.

PLAIN GOOD BAGELS
1 to 1-1/2 cups oat flour
1 cup plain oat bran
1 cup whole grain wheat flour
1 cup vital wheat gluten
1-1/3 cups warm water
1/2 cup melted butter
2 eggs
1/2 tsp. salt
2 Tb. granular Splenda™
2-1/4 tsp. dry active yeast (reduce by 1/2 tsp. @ high altitudes)
Makes 18 whole bagels - per HALF bagel: 51 cal, 1 g fat (0 sat), 7 g carb (1 g fiber), 4 g protein

BLUEBERRY: Add 1 cup dried, unsweetened blueberries and total of 1/2 cup granular Splenda™ (instead of only 2 Tb.) to plain good dough. *Makes 18 whole bagels - per HALF bagel: 67 cal, 1 g fat (0 sat), 11 g carb (2 g fiber), 4 g protein*

CRANBERRY ORANGE:
Add 1/2 cup dried, chopped, unsweetened cranberries, 1 tsp. dried orange peel, 1 tsp. orange extract, and a total of 1/2 cup granular Splenda™ to plain good dough. *Makes 18 whole bagels - per HALF bagel: 61 cal, 1 g fat (0 sat), 10 g carb (1 g fiber), 4 g protein*

ONION: Add 3 Tb. finely minced fresh onion and 1 Tb. onion powder to dough. After boiling bagels, brush tops with 1 beaten egg yolk and sprinkle with 2 Tb. additional dry onion flakes, pushing flakes down into the yolk to help them adhere better. *Makes 18 bagels - per HALF bagel: 55 cal, 1 g fat (0 sat), 8 g carb (1 g fiber), 4 g protein*

EVERYTHING: Add 2 tsp. minced garlic, 1/3 cup shredded cheddar cheese, and 1/4 cup minced raw sunflower seeds or almonds to onion bagel dough. *Makes 18 whole bagels - per HALF bagel: 76 cal, 2 g fat (0 sat), 10 g carb (1 g fiber), 4 g protein*

Bars

CHOCO-CHUNK

1 cup unsweetened peanut butter
1 cup butter, softened
1 cup granular Splenda™
2 eggs
1/4 cup SF syrup (any flavor)
2-1/2 cups TLC Bake mix
1/2 cup unsalted peanuts, coarsely chopped
6 oz. SF chocolate, coarsely chopped

Preheat oven to 350 F. Grease or line a 13x9 pan. Cream peanut butter, butter, syrup, and Splenda. Beat in eggs, followed by bake mix. Spread into prepared pan. Sprinkle chocolate chunks and peanut pieces evenly over top of batter. Bake for 20- 25 minutes, until done. *Makes 24 bars - per each: 249 cal, 20 g fat (7 sat), 11 g carb (2 g fiber, 2 g SA), 8 g protein*

ENERGY BARS

1 cup butter
4 Tb. unsweetened peanut butter (or any nut butter)
1 cup SF syrup (any flavor desired)
3/4 cup maltitol syrup
1-1/2 cups walnuts, chopped (any nut will do)
1-1/2 cups unsalted roasted peanuts, coarsely chopped (again, any nut will do)
1-1/2 cups unsweetened grated coconut
3 cups plain puffed rice or millet
1/2 cup flax meal
1/2 cup unsalted sunflower kernels
1 cup dried unsweetened cranberries
4 cups protein powder (any flavor)

Melt butter; stir in nut butter, flavorings, and syrups. Set aside. Combine nuts with coconut, puffed rice, flax meal, sunflower kernels, and cranberries. Add wet ingredients, then slowly work in protein powder, mixing well. Press firmly into a 7x11 or 9x9 pan, and chill for at least 6 hours before cutting. I wrap these individually and store refrigerated up to two weeks. *20 servings - per each: 305 cal, 21 g fat (7 sat.), 12 g carb (2 g fiber, 3 g SA), 18 g protein.*

FABULOUS FAKES

VARIATIONS: Endless! Try adding different flavoring extracts and omitting the nut butter. Skipping the dried fruit will reduce carbs by just 1 per serving, or you can double the amount for just 1 added carb per serving. Using 1 cup dried unsweetened blueberries instead of the cranberries adds 2 carbs per serving, and using apricots adds 3 carbs.

GERMAN CHOCOLATE BROWNIES
1 cup unsalted butter
1-1/2 oz. unsweetened baking chocolate
1 cup chocolate flavored SF syrup
1/2 cup granular Splenda™
3 large eggs
2 cups unsweetened coconut, divided
1 cup almond flour (any nut meal will do)
1 cup chocolate protein powder
1 cup chopped walnuts
Preheat oven to 350 F and grease or line a 13x9 pan. Melt chocolate and butter together. Beat in syrup, then add eggs, followed by one cup of the coconut, the nut meal, protein powder, and lastly fold in the chopped nuts. Do not over mix. Bake for 20 minutes. Cool for 5 minutes before proceeding with topping.

TOPPING: While baking the brownies, toast the remaining 1 cup coconut in a separate pan until nicely golden, about 10 minutes.
8 oz. cream cheese
2 Tb. vanilla or coconut flavored SF syrup
2 tsp. vanilla extract
1/3 cup granular Splenda™
1 cup chopped walnuts
2 Tb. additional granular Splenda™
Melt the cream cheese with syrup, then whisk in extract and Splenda until smooth. Pour/spread warm frosting evenly over warm brownies, then sprinkle toasted coconut, chopped nuts, and 2 Tb. sweetener over frosting. Press everything down gently, to make it stick better, then place pan under broiler just until everything browns slightly. Cool thoroughly.
24 servings - per each: 248 cal, 23 g fat (8 g sat.), 5 g carb (2 g fiber), 7 g protein

LEMON MELTAWAYS

1 cup granular Splenda™, divided
1/2 cup cold butter
1/2 cup vanilla protein powder
1/2 cup almond flour

2 eggs
1 cup granular Splenda™
3 Tb. lemon juice
2 tsp. lemon zest
1 Tb. ThickenThin NotStarch™ or 1 tsp guar gum
pinch of salt

Preheat oven to 350° F. Place 4 Tb. of Splenda in a food processor and process until it powders. Remove and reserve for topping.

Make crust: place remaining 3/4 cup Splenda into food processor and whiz until it powders. Add the cold butter, cut up into small pieces, along with the protein powder and almond flour and pulse to combine. Press into bottom of a 9 inch square or 7x11 oblong pan. Bake approximately 20 minutes until lightly browned.

Meanwhile, combine the eggs with the other 1 cup Splenda, and process until smooth. Add remaining ingredients while the machine is still running, and process until smooth and thick.

When the bottom is baked (right out of the oven), pour the topping over it, then return to oven for about 25 more minutes.

Remove from oven, cool, and sprinkle with reserved powdered Splenda.

12 servings, each: 171 cal, 14 g fat (5 sat), 7 g carb (1 g fiber), 5 g protein

I just <u>love </u>that this decadent two-step dessert is so easy and makes barely any mess in the kitchen.

VARIATION: Use orange zest and extract to taste in place of lemon peel and juice. May add some orange food coloring if desired, to make this variation look just right.

ORANGE CRANBERRY SQUARES

1 cup plus 2 Tb. SF syrup, divided (orange flavor recommended but you can use vanilla or another flavor)
1 cup dried, unsweetened cranberries
4 eggs
24 oz. cream cheese, divided
1 cup plus 2 Tb. granular Splenda™, divided
1 cup plus 3 Tb. vanilla protein powder, divided
2 cups almond flour or other nut meal
2 tsp. orange extract (more to taste when using vanilla or other syrup flavors)

One hour before beginning this recipe:
Bring 1 cup of syrup to a boil, add cranberries carefully, stir; set aside to soften. Take eggs out of refrigerator and set on the counter to come to room
temperature. Take the cream cheese out of the packages and cut it into 10-12 chunks per pkg; set aside.

Preheat oven to 375 F. Separate eggs, adding whites
to mixer bowl and setting aside the yolks as follows:
1 yolk and three yolks (in separate containers). Beat
egg whites until frothy; add 1/2 cup Splenda; beat
until they turn solid white and then for one additional minute. By hand, fold in the 1 cup protein
powder and the nut meal. As soon as it comes together, use wet fingers to spread out in well-greased
or lined 13x9 pan. Place in oven for 8 minutes.
While this crust bakes, add the 3 egg yolks to the
mixer bowl along with the extract and the remaining
half cup Splenda; beat till thickened and blended.
Start adding cream cheese chunks. Mixture should
be lumpy and thick! Do not over beat. Fold in the still
warm cranberries and syrup. Spread mixture gently
over warm crust.
Take the remaining yolk, add remaining 2 Tb. SF
syrup and 3 Tb. protein powder and mix. May add
food coloring if desired. Spoon and drizzle this out
over the top of the cream cheese and berry batter in
a decorative manner. Bake for 40 more minutes.
*24 servings - per each: 249 cal, 21 g fat (6 sat), 7 g
carb (2 g fiber), 10 g protein*

S'MORES BARS

3 cups unsweetened flaked coconut
2/3 cup whole rolled oats
2/3 cup vanilla protein powder
1 cup oat flour
2 eggs
1 cup softened butter
1/2 cup SF syrup (caramel flavor recommended)
1/2 cup granular Splenda™
6 oz. SF chocolate bars, chopped coarsely
1 cup chopped pecans or other nuts
4 Tb. powdered egg white
1/4 cup maltitol syrup
1/2 cup SF syrup (toasted marshmallow flavor recommended for ultimate results)

Toast coconut at 350 F for about ten minutes, until a deep golden brown. Cool slightly, then puree in a food processor until it takes on the consistency of wet sand. Scrape out into a bowl and mix with oats, protein powder, and oat flour. Set aside.

Put butter in bowl of food processor and pulse to cream. Slowly add first 1/2 cup of the SF syrup, the Splenda, and then the eggs. Add reserved dry ingredients in three batches, pulsing briefly after each addition. Scrape batter out into a greased 13x9 pan and smooth the top. Sprinkle with chocolate and nuts, then bake at 350 for 15 minutes.

While base is baking, heat last 1/2 cup SF syrup and maltitol syrup to almost boiling. Use a fork to add dry egg white powder slowly, and stir vigorously to break it up. Allow to rest for 2 minutes, then place in mixer bowl and whip until soft peaks form.

Spread egg white mixture gently over the pre-baked base, immediately reduce oven temp. to 275 F, and return pan to oven for another 15-20 minutes, until lightly golden on top.

24 servings - per each: 209 cal, 17 g fat (9 g sat), 11 g carb (2 g fiber, 3 g sugar alcohols), 4 g protein

SOMOA BARS

3 cups unsweetened flaked coconut
1/3 cup rolled oats
1/2 cup vanilla protein powder
2/3 cup granular Splenda™
1 cup butter, softened
1/2 cup coconut flavored SF syrup
1 egg
1 cup sliced almonds
6 oz. SF chocolate bars, chopped coarsely
1 cup pecans
1 egg
1 cup heavy cream
1/3 cup maltitol syrup

Toast coconut at 350 F for about ten minutes, until a deep golden brown. Cool slightly, then puree in a food processor until it takes on the consistency of wet sand. Transfer pureed coconut to a mixing bowl and add the oats, protein powder, and Splenda. Use a whisk to break up any clumps, and mix well. Remove 2 cups; set aside. Add butter to the remaining coconut mixture in the bowl, and cream. Slowly add syrup, then egg. Scrape batter out into a greased 13x9 pan. Sprinkle with sliced almonds. Place broken up chocolate bars and pecans in processor and pulse to coarse chunks. Sprinkle over almonds, followed by the reserved coconut mixture. Beat cream, egg, and maltitol syrup together. Pour slowly over the layers already in pan. Place in oven and immediately reduce heat to 325 F. Bake for 40 minutes until a deep golden; cool to room temperature on a rack; then refrigerate. (You may see butter bubbling up from the edges when removing from oven; this is normal and to be expected.)

36 servings- per each: 164 cal, 15 g fat (7 g sat), 6 g carb (1 g fiber, 2 g SA), 2 g protein

These are very rich, and I find that cutting them into 36 servings is appropriate, even though that is an unusual serving size for my dessert recipes.

Cakes & Cupcakes

ANY FLAVOR

1 cup softened butter
6 oz. softened cream cheese
1 cup granular Splenda™
6 eggs
2 Tb. vanilla extract (or use any other flavor and adjust amounts as needed)
1 cup SF syrup (any flavor you desire)
2 cups + 1 Tb. protein powder (soy or whey, any flavor you desire)
2 cups any type nut meal (almond flour calculated)
1 Tb. baking powder (2-1/4 tsp. @ high altitude)

Preheat oven to 350 F. Grease cake pans well, then dust with the 1 Tb. protein powder.

Cream butter, cream cheese, and sweetener well. Add eggs, one at a time, beating well after each addition. Add extract and flavored syrup, and beat on low until creamy and well mixed. Fold in protein powder, nut flour, and baking powder. Pour into prepared pan(s). Bake until a toothpick inserted into center comes out clean – about 30-40 minutes for a 13x9 snack cake, 15-20 minutes for two rounds or 18-20 minutes for cupcakes – longer if you use a soy protein powder, shorter if you use one that is whey-based.

18 servings - per each: 294 cal, 25 g fat (9 g sat), 6 g carb (1 g fiber), 13 g protein

VARIATIONS: Vary this recipe as much as you like - if using strawberry protein powder and syrup, I add a cup of minced fresh or frozen strawberries, as well... almond syrup with almond extract and toasted almonds... chocolate protein powder with hazelnut or cherry syrup - get creative! The following variations are fabulous with spice flavored syrup:

CARROT CAKE: Add 1 cup lightly packed, grated carrot (4-6 average carrots) *18 servings: 304 cal, 25 g fat (9 g sat), 8 g carb (2 g fiber), 14 g protein, each*

ZUCCHINI: Add 2 cups grated zucchini (1 small one, unpeeled) *18 servings: 294 cal, 25 g fat (9 g sat), 6 g carb (2 g fiber), 14 g protein, each*

BLUEBERRY CRUNCH CAKE

1/4 cup coconut oil or softened butter
1/4 cup mayonnaise
1/2 cup granular Splenda™
1 egg
1/2 cup vanilla protein powder
1/4 cup oat flour
2 Tb. dry whole milk
1/2 cup buttermilk
1 tsp. vanilla extract
1 cup blueberries (or raspberries)
1 cup walnuts, chopped finely
1/2 cup flax meal
1/2 tsp. cinnamon
2 Tb. melted butter

Preheat oven to 350 F and grease a 9x9 or 8x8 baking pan well. Cream oil or butter with mayonnaise, Splenda, and egg. Stop mixer and sprinkle whey powder, oat flour, and dry milk powder over creamed mixture. Pour buttermilk and vanilla extract over dry ingredients. Turn mixer to low and blend just till mixed (may be lumpy). Scrape batter out into prepared pan and smooth top.

Sprinkle blueberries evenly over batter. Mix melted butter with nuts, flax meal, and cinnamon, and sprinkle evenly over berries.

Bake for about 40 minutes, until cake is cooked through and topping is a deep golden brown.

12 servings - per each: 221 cal, 18 g fat (6 sat), 7 g carb (1 g fiber), 7 g protein.

Did you know ...

Blueberries are rich in vitamin C, iron, magnesium, and antioxidants.

Do not wash blueberries before refrigerating (the water will hasten spoilage), or before freezing (the water will make the skins tough). Rinse frozen blueberries after thawing instead, and wash fresh berries just before use.

CHERRY CORDIAL CAKE

CAKE LAYER:

1 cup unsweetened cocoa powder
3 cups almond flour or other nut meal
1/2 cup + 1 Tb. chocolate protein powder
1 Tb. baking powder (2-1/4 tsp. @ high altitude)
4 eggs
1 cup butter, melted
1 can SF Cherry Pie Filling (20 oz., this analysis based on using Lucky Leaf™ brand)
1/2 cup SF syrup (chocolate, cherry, or a combo)

Preheat oven to 350 F. Generously grease a 13x9 pan, then use the 1 Tb. of protein powder to "flour" it. Whisk together the cocoa, nut meal, remaining protein powder, and baking powder; set aside.

Beat the eggs well, and slowly add the melted butter, followed by the pie filling and syrup. Add dry ingredients; blend and turn out into prepared pan. Bake for 25-35 minutes until it tests done.

PUDDING LAYER:

1/2 cup cocoa powder
4 Tb. Thicken NotStarch™ or 4 tsp. guar gum
pinch salt
3 eggs
2 cups half and half cream
1 cup SF chocolate syrup
2 Tb. butter
1 tsp. vanilla extract

Place cocoa, starch and salt in saucepan and whisk together. Beat in eggs, then slowly beat in the liquid over medium heat. Continue to cook, stirring constantly, until mixture thickens and comes to a full rolling boil for one minute. Remove from heat and stir in butter and vanilla. Turn hot pudding out over surface of hot or cool cake layer, smooth surface, and cover with plastic wrap to prevent formation of a skin. Once partially cool, refrigerate to chill.

TOP LAYER

Additional 20 oz. can SF Cherry Pie Filling

When cake and pudding are well-chilled, spread another can of pie filling over top of the pudding.

24 servings - per each: 337 calories, 29 g fat (7 sat), 14 g carb (6 g fiber), 11 protein

DUMP CAKE

2 Tb. unsalted butter
1 oz. unsweetened baking chocolate (optional)
1/2 cup heavy cream
1 tsp. vanilla extract
1-1/4 cups granular Splenda™, divided
1 cup protein powder (any flavor)
1/2 cup almond flour
1/4 cup vital wheat gluten
1-1/2 tsp. baking powder (1 tsp. @ high altitude)
1/4 tsp. salt
2 Tb. cocoa powder (optional)
1 cup boiling Davinci syrup (any flavor)

Preheat oven to 350 degrees and grease a 9 inch square or round pan very well. Melt butter, add baking chocolate if using, and stir until chocolate melts. Add cream and vanilla and beat until smooth and well mixed.

In a separate bowl, mix 3/4 cup of the Splenda with the protein powder, almond flour, gluten, baking powder, and salt. Add cream mixture; mix well, and then spread out evenly into prepared pan. (Batter will be very thick. If too thick to spread, add additional cream one tablespoon at a time as needed.)

Sprinkle batter with remaining 1/2 cup Splenda, then cocoa powder. Pour boiling syrup slowly over all. DO NOT MIX. Bake for 30 minutes. Serve warm with whipped heavy cream, or cool, split, and frost.

8 servings - per each: 228 cal, 16 g fat (5 g sat), 9 g carb (2 g fiber), 13 g protein

VARIATIONS: Many!!! This was originally created in chocolate, but I have varied it many different ways since then. All vanilla is delicious, as is lemon with vanilla syrup and poppy seeds on top. Try orange syrup with vanilla protein powder and dried orange peel over the top. How about using almond syrup with crushed almond pieces over the top?

Substitute 1-3/4 cups TLC bake mix for protein powder, almond flour, baking powder, gluten, and salt:
8 servings - per each: 199 cal, 13 g fat (5 g sat), 12 g carb (3 g fiber), 10 g protein

ORANGE DREAM CAKE

Because the individual components of this cake may be enjoyed by themselves or in other dessert combinations, individual nutrition data is provided for each component, as well as totals at the end which include everything called for in the assembled cake., which I originally created for my 38th birthday.

CITRUS SPONGE CAKE

10 large eggs, separated
pinch salt
3 Tb. warm water
1 Tb. Grand Marnier™ liqueur
1 cup granular Splenda™
2 tsp. dried orange peel
1/4 cup vital wheat gluten
1/2 cup oat flour
3/4 cup vanilla protein powder

For best results, allow eggs to come to room temperature before beginning.

Preheat oven to 325 F. Grease two round cake pans well, and "flour" pans with 1 Tb. of the protein powder. Separate eggs. Whip whites in clean bowl with pinch of salt until stiff; set aside. Whisk together orange peel, gluten, oat flour, and protein powder; set aside. Beat egg yolks with Grand Marnier, water, and Splenda, scraping sides as needed. Add reserved dry ingredients; beat just until blended. Add about one fourth of the reserved egg whites and mix well to lighten. Scrape this mixture out atop the beaten egg whites; gently fold together just until mixed.

Divide batter evenly between the prepared pans and bake for approximately 20 minutes, until lightly golden. Remove cakes from pans promptly, and cool on a rack.

While baking cake layers, toast the pecans for the top layer in a separate pan. Keep an eye on them so they don't burn, since times can vary depending on the oil content of nuts, but mine were perfect when baked for the same time as the layers.

12 servings - per each: 127 cal, 5 g fat (1 g sat), 8 g carb, 10 g protein

INSTANT ORANGE CURD

1/4 cup granular Splenda™
1-1/2 tsp. dried orange peel
1-1/2 tsp. guar gum or 1 Tb. Thickenthin Notstarch™
1 cup orange flavored SF syrup, heated to boiling

Place Splenda, orange peel and guar gum in blender or food processor and process until fine. Add hot syrup slowly while machine is running; process until thickened.

Makes 1 cup - per 1/4 cup: 18 cal, 4.5 g carb

CINNAMON-PECAN TOPPING

1 cup whole pecans, toasted
1 cup granular Splenda™, divided
1/2 tsp. ground cinnamon
8 oz. cream cheese, softened
1 Tb. Grand Marnier™ liqueur (optional)
3 Tb. heavy whipping cream

When the pecans are toasted and warm, toss them with the cinnamon and 1/4 cup Splenda. To complete topping, fish the cinnamon dusted pecans out of the cinnamon and Splenda and set them aside. Beat the cream cheese until smooth, scraping sides as needed; add heavy cream, Grand Marnier, cinnamon mixture, and finally the remaining Splenda. Whip until smooth.

Makes 1-1/4 cups - per 1/4 cup: 340 calories, 32 g fat (12 g sat), 10 g carb, 4 g protein

FINAL ASSEMBLY, COMPLETE CAKE:

Place one layer on serving plate and spread with the curd. Place second layer upside-down atop curd, and spread with topping. Sprinkle pecans over all, and press gently down into topping to adhere. Store refrigerated.

12 servings - per each: 289 cal, 18 g fat (6 g sat), 17 g carb, 13 g protein

VARIATION: Omit orange curd in favor of two layers of cinnamon pecan topping (double the topping recipe, and chop the pecans in the middle layer finely).

12 servings - per each: 410 cal, 32 g fat (12 g sat), 17 g carb, 14 g protein

WHOOPIE PIES

1-1/2 cups mayonnaise
1 cup SF syrup (any flavor desired)
1 tsp. vanilla or other extract/flavorings
and/or 5 Tb. cocoa powder (optional)
and/or 1/4 cup nut butter (optional)
1 cup oat flour
1/2 cup vital wheat gluten
1 cup protein powder (any flavor desired)
2 tsp. baking soda (1-2/3 tsp. @ high altitude)
1/2 tsp. salt

Preheat oven to 350 F. Line two large baking sheets with parchment paper or grease very well and dust with protein powder. Whip mayonnaise, sugar free syrup, and liquid flavorings, if using, until smooth. Sprinkle cocoa powder (if using) over top of mixture, followed by remaining dry ingredients. Blend until smooth. Divide into 32 small mounds. (I like to use a disposable pastry bag to pipe the batter out, but you can spoon out dollops, too.) Bake 8-10 minutes, until lightly browned. Cool briefly before filling.

FILLING:
8 oz. softened cream cheese
2 Tb. hot water
1 cup granular Splenda™
1-2 tsp. vanilla extract or other flavoring
2 Tb. cream

While batter is baking, beat cream cheese on low until smooth. Slowly add remaining ingredients, then beat on high speed until fluffy, scraping sides as needed.

Spread flat side of one mini-cake with generous amount of filling, then top with an additional cake. Wrap each sandwich individually in plastic wrap and refrigerate. They won't last long, and do freeze well. *You just may find that half of one of these at a time is plenty. 16 servings - per each: 359 cal, 29 g fat (6 g sat), 9 g carb (1 g fiber), 9 g protein*

VARIATION: Use a batch of the marshmallow cream on page 114 for the filling, instead. *16 servings - per each: 359 cal, 24 g fat (3 g sat), 20 g carb (1 g fiber, 13 g SA), 9 g protein*

FABULOUS FAKES

Cereal: Hot

I love cereal. Going low carb means you have to make your own most of the time, but it doesn't mean you have to do without!

BASIC HOT FLAX CEREAL
1/2 cup oat bran
1/2 cup almond flour or other nut meal
1/2 cup wheat bran
1 cup flax meal
1 cup vanilla protein powder
Simply mix thoroughly and store refrigerated.
To prepare one serving, blend 1/2 cup dry mix with 1/2 cup boiling water. Stir and boil for two minutes, adding additional water slowly until desired consistency is attained. *Makes 3-1/2 cups dry - per 1/2 cup: 276 cal, 18 g fat (1 g sat), 16 g carb (8 g fiber), 19 g protein*

FLAX FREE HOT CEREAL:
1 cup grated unsweetened coconut
1 cup vanilla protein powder
1 cup walnuts, chopped
1/2 cup wheat bran
6 Tb. oat bran
2 tsp. guar gum or 2 Tb. ThickenThin Notstarch™
Makes 4 cups - per 1/2 cup: 189 cal, 14 g fat (3 g sat), 9 g carb (5 g fiber), 10 g protein.
Prepare as above, but mix 1/2 cup dry mix with just 1/4 cup water to start, and adjust to taste from there.

VARIATIONS: Endless! By substituting SF syrup for the water, you can vary the taste and sweetness considerably without affecting the carb count at all. Why not add some chopped nuts or seeds for more texture, and if you can afford the carbs, some unsweetened dried fruits? I like adding chopped pecans and preparing it with SF maple syrup or extract. Walnuts with banana flavoring is another favorite. You can top this with cream, sour cream, yogurt, chopped fruit or nuts, etc.

Cereal: Easy Granola

2 cups whole, rolled oats (old-fashioned)
2 cups sliced almonds (or chopped walnuts)
1 cup whole pecans (or other favorite nut or seed)
2-1/2 cups grated, unsweetened coconut
1 cup flax meal
1/2 cup unsalted pumpkin kernels (or sunflower)
1/2 cup oat bran
1/3 cup steel cut oats (or use additional oat bran)
1 Tb. psyllium husk powder
2 Tb. cinnamon
1 tsp. nutmeg
1 cup SF vanilla syrup
1 cup granular Splenda™
1/3 cup oil
1-3/4 cups egg whites (a 16 oz. carton works great)

Toss the grains, seeds, nuts, brans and spices together in a large bowl. Whisk the egg whites in a separate bowl with the syrup, Splenda, and oil. Pour liquid ingredients slowly over dry ones, tossing until evenly moistened. Divide between several large shallow pans lined with foil and bake at 250 F for 2-1/2 to 3 hours, stirring mixture every 30 minutes. You may need to bake longer if in a humid climate; make sure it is completely dry throughout the largest clumps before allowing it to cool, then storing it in an airtight container. *You could bake this for a shorter time at a higher temp, but this way is practically fool-proof.

Makes 14 cups - per half cup: 188 cal, 14 g fat (2 sat), 12 g carb (4 g fiber), 6 g protein

RECIPE NOTES: You can vary this recipe easily. Delicious with dried fruits added! If you can find coconut flakes, substitute some of those for part of the grated coconut that is called for. Use this for snacking, cereal, or sprinkle over yogurt along with fresh or dried berries. The bulk fiber in this recipe causes expansion and a large yield. I prefer to vacuum seal individual portions of this delicious treat so I don't get carried away with it!

Cheesecakes

BASIC NUT CRUST

3 cups almond flour
1/3 cup granular Splenda™ (or more to taste)
2 egg whites

Preheat oven to 450 degrees F. Mix almond flour and Splenda in spring-form pan. Add beaten egg white and mix well. Press evenly into bottom and up sides of pan with wet fingers. Place pan in freezer to chill while preparing filling.

BASIC CHEESECAKE

2 lbs. softened cream cheese (4 packages)
2 eggs
1-1/2 cups granular Splenda™
1 tsp. vanilla extract
1/2 tsp. almond extract
1 cup sour cream

Beat room temperature cream cheese until very smooth, scraping down beaters and sides of bowl at least once. Slowly add the Splenda, beating well. Add eggs, one at a time, scraping sides and beating well after each addition. Add the sour cream and extracts and mix well. Pour into chilled crust and bake at 450 degrees F for 10 minutes. Reduce oven temperature to 250 degrees F and bake another 50 minutes. Cool on a rack until it reaches room temperature, then place in refrigerator to thoroughly chill. Once chilled, remove pan sides.

16 servings - per each: 411 cal, 38 g fat (14 g sat), 10 g carb (3 g fiber), 12 g protein (including crust)

RECIPE NOTES: This recipe works best in a 10" spring-form pan. Allow ingredients to come to room temperature before beginning. Do mix well, but don't over mix the batter - too much air in the batter can cause surface cracks in the finished product. Do scrape the bowl often and insure that you have no lumps at any step in this process. Cheesecakes freeze really well - just slice and wrap individual portions tightly.

LEMON YOGURT CHEESECAKE: Prepare as for Basic, but substitute 1-1/2 cups plain yogurt for the 1 cup sour cream, and omit the extracts in favor of the peel and juice from 1 lemon. Add 1/3 cup vanilla protein powder and increase Splenda to 1-1/2 cups. *16 servings - per each: 406 cal, 35 g fat (12 g sat), 12 g carb (3 g fiber), 14 g protein* (including crust)

ORANGE BLOSSOM CHEESECAKE: Prepare lemon cheesecake but substitute 2 tsp. orange extract and 1 tsp. dried or fresh orange peel for lemon juice/ blend 1 egg yolk with 1/2 cup protein powder and 1/2 cup orange flavored SF syrup, and spread evenly over top of cheesecake batter before baking. *16 servings - per each: 511 cal, 46 g fat (14 g sat), 13 g carb (5 g fiber), 17 g protein* (including crust)

Toasted Coconut Cheesecake

CRUST
2 cups grated, unsweetened coconut
1/2 cup oat flour
1/2 cup granular Splenda™
6 Tb. cold butter, in chunks
Heat oven to 400 F. Spread coconut out in a shallow pan and toast, stirring once or twice, just until it turns golden. Add oat flour and Splenda, mix, then cut butter in until mixture resembles wet sand. Press firmly in bottom of a 10" spring-form pan and bake about ten minutes, until golden brown.
CHEESECAKE
2 lbs. softened cream cheese (4 packages)
1 cup granular Splenda™
1/2 - 1 tsp. coconut flavoring (start with less)
1/2 cup SF syrup (if coconut, can reduce extract)
1/3 cup vanilla or plain flavored protein powder
2 eggs
Mix ingredients in order listed, tasting and adjusting batter prior to adding the eggs. Pour over warm crust and put back in the 400 F oven for five minutes; reduce heat to 250 F; continue baking for another 45 minutes. *16 servings - per each: 300 cal, 28 g fat (17 g sat), 7 g carb (1 g fiber), 7 g protein*

Cookies

CHOCOLATE CHUNK
1/2 cup butter
4 oz. cream cheese
1-1/4 cups granular Splenda™
2-1/2 cups TLC bake mix
2 eggs
1/4 cup vanilla flavored SF syrup
6 oz. SF chocolate bars, chopped into chunks
Preheat oven to 350 F. Cut butter and cream cheese into Splenda and bake mix with pastry cutter or two knives. Beat eggs and SF syrup separately; toss with butter mixture gently until blended. Fold in bake mix and chocolate pieces. Drop by rounded teaspoonful onto lined or well greased baking sheets and bake for 12-15 minutes, until lightly golden on edges. Cool on racks. Wrap tightly and refrigerate once cool.
Makes 36 - per cookie: 93 cal, 7 g fat (3 g sat), 5 g carb (1 g fiber, 1 g SA), 3 g protein

CINNAMON WEDDING COOKIES
1 cup granular Splenda™, divided
3-1/2 tsp. ground cinnamon, divided
2 cup walnuts
2 egg whites
6 Tb. protein powder
Preheat oven to 325 F and line or grease a baking sheet. Place 1/4 cup of the Splenda in a food processor and pulse until powdered; remove and reserve. Place remaining 3/4 cup of Splenda in the food processor with 3 tsp. of the cinnamon and the walnuts, and grind finely. Remove and reserve. Add egg whites to food processor and whip. Stop machine, scrape sides, add fold in protein powder and reserved ground walnut mixture. With wet hands or ice cream scoop, form 15 golf ball sized cookies. Bake for 20 minutes until just dry to the touch. Cool for 2-3 minutes. Combine last 1/2 tsp. cinnamon with reserved powdered Splenda in a small bag. Place warm cookies in bag a few at a time, and shake to coat.
Makes 15 - per each: 102 cal, 8 g fat (0 sat), 3 g carb, 5 g protein

CLASSIC CUTOUT COOKIES
1 cup almond flour
1 cup protein isolate (soy or wheat)
1 cup vanilla flavored protein powder
1/2 tsp. baking soda
3/4 tsp. baking powder (1/2 tsp. @ altitude)
1/8 tsp. salt
1/2 cup softened butter
1 cup palm oil (or coconut oil or additional butter)
1 cup granular Splenda™
2 eggs
1/3 cup maltitol syrup
1 tsp. vanilla extract

Combine first 6 ingredients and set aside. Cream butter, palm oil, and Splenda. Beat in eggs and syrups, then fold in reserved dry ingredients. Wrap tightly and chill at least one hour. Roll out thinly, cut into shapes, and bake at 375 F until lightly golden on edges (times can vary greatly depending on size of cookies and thickness of dough).

Makes 48 - per cookie: 103 cal, 9 g fat (3 g sat), 3 g carb, 4 g protein

ALL-PURPOSE ICING & GLAZE
4 cups granular Splenda™ OR 2 cups powdered
maltitol - If using Splenda, powder it first, which will reduce it to about 2 cups.
3 Tb. softened butter
1/2 tsp. vanilla extract
1-3 Tb. cream

Cream butter with sweetener and vanilla. Slowly add cream until desired consistency is attained. Excellent over lots of things!!

@ Yield of 48 - with Splenda: 15 cal, 0.8 g fat, 2 g carb, each. With maltitol powder, 21 cal, 0.8 g fat, 3 g carb (3 g SA)

Entire batch - with Splenda: 735 cal, 38 g fat (23 g sat), 97 g carb, 1 g protein. With maltitol: 987 cal, 38 g fat (23 g sat), 160 g carb (159 g SA), 1 g protein

VARIATIONS: Add food coloring(s) as desired. Use lemon juice instead of cream, and sprinkle with poppy seeds.

MAGIC MERINGUES
3/4 cup granular Splenda™
1/4 cup unsweetened cocoa powder (optional)
3 Tb. TLC bake mix
2 tsp. guar gum or 2 Tb. ThickenThin Notstarch™
2 tsp. ground cinnamon (optional)
1 tsp. vanilla extract (can use other flavorings)
1/2 cup maltitol syrup
4 egg whites
Pinch salt

Preheat oven to 300 F. Whisk first five ingredients together and set aside. Bring maltitol syrup to boiling point. Add vanilla extract and set aside. Beat egg whites and salt at high speed until soft peaks form. Slowly add boiling syrup in a thin stream, while continuing to beat, until glossy with stiff peaks but not dry. Stop mixer and fold in reserved dry ingredients gently. Spoon or pipe one inch diameter dollops onto parchment paper or silicone lined baking sheets. Bake for ninety minutes; turn oven off and leave baking sheets in closed oven for an additional four hours, or until completely cooled and crisp throughout. *Makes 24 - per each: 20 cal, 0.2 g fat, 3 g carb (2 g SA)*
VARIATION: Bake in a 13x9 pan - comes out like a chewy, sticky brownie!

NUT CRUNCHERS
1 cup sliced almonds (or other unsalted, sliced nut)
1/2 cup chopped walnuts (or other unsalted nut)
1/2 cup unsweetened, grated coconut
1 cup granular Splenda™
1 tsp. ground cinnamon
1/4 tsp. nutmeg
1/4 tsp. salt
2 eggs, beaten
1 tsp. vanilla extract

Preheat oven to 400 F. Toss first seven ingredients together. Beat eggs with vanilla; add to dry mix. Drop by heaping teaspoonfuls onto a well-greased or lined baking sheet. Bake for about 15 minutes, until golden brown on edges. *Makes 15 - per each: 86 cal, 7 g fat (1 sat), 3 g carb (1 g fiber), 3 g protein*

OATMEAL COOKIES

2/3 cup palm oil (or use coconut oil, butter, etc.)
1/3 cup mayonnaise
1-1/2 cups granular Splenda™
1 egg
1 tsp. vanilla or maple extract
1 tsp. baking powder (reduce to 3/4 tsp. @ altitude)
1/4 tsp. baking soda
1 cup vanilla protein powder
3 cups almond flour
1 cup wheat bran
2 cups cold, prepared Irish steel cut oats (1/2 cup dry oats plus 2 c. water, simmer till water is absorbed; cover and allow to rest until fully soft. I do this the night before so it can sit all night.)
1 cup dried, unsweetened blueberries or cranberries (optional - but definitely the crowning touch)

Cream the palm oil with the mayonnaise and Splenda. Add the egg and desired flavoring extract, then reduce speed to low and add remaining ingredients in order listed.
ALLOW BATTER TO SIT ON COUNTER AND REST FOR 30 MINUTES. (I accidentally discovered that this changes the texture and appearance of the finished cookies to much more closely resemble 'real' oatmeal cookies!)
Heat oven to 375 F. Drop by teaspoonful onto greased or lined baking sheets. Bake for 15-20 minutes, until deep golden brown on bottom and edges.

Makes 48
Per cookie, without any fruit: 149 cal, 12.5 g fat (1 g sat.), 5 g carb (2 g fiber), 5 g protein.
Per cookie, made with blueberries: 155 cal, 12.5 g fat (1 g sat.), 7 g carb (2 g fiber), 4 g protein.
Per cookie, made with cranberries: 150 cal, 12.5 g fat (1 g sat.), 6 g carb (2 g fiber), 4 g protein.

RECIPE NOTES: The Nut Crunchers on the previous page remind me of oatmeal cookies, too, strange as that sounds... if you are an oatmeal fan, be sure to try that recipe, too.

Flatbread

1/2 cup wheat bran
2/3-1 cup chicken broth
1/2 cup protein isolate (soy or wheat)
4 Tb. garbanzo bean flour (or whole wheat)
2 Tb. vital wheat gluten
2 Tb. oat flour
1/2 tsp. onion powder
1/4 tsp. garlic powder
1 tsp. granular Splenda™
1 tsp. salt
1 tsp. baking powder
2 Tb. palm or coconut oil (could use butter)

Stir wheat bran into 1/2 cup of the broth and set aside to soak for ten minutes before proceeding. Place all dry ingredients in a mixing bowl and whisk together. Cut in palm oil using pastry cutter, two knives, or your fingers. Stir in softened wheat bran, then add reserved broth slowly, adding just as needed so that you can form a smooth ball of dough.

Cover and allow to rest for ten minutes, while heating a heavy pan over medium-low heat (I prefer cast iron, but anything will work).

Divide dough into 12 equal portions and roll each into a small, thin disk. Dough will be sticky - I used a nonstick baking mat and flattened the dough out with my palm, then smoothed all the edges before scraping the formed disk up with a pastry cutter (or the side of a wide knife).

Cook slowly, a few at a time, in the preheated ungreased frying pan until golden on each side and cooked through in center, four to six minutes depending on thickness.

12 servings - per each: 64 cal, 3 g fat (1 g sat), 4 g carb (1 g fiber), 6 g protein

RECIPE NOTES: These hold together very well, making them suitable for burgers or sandwiches, and with carbs this low, you can easily eat two at a time! Could use water in place of chicken stock, too.

PIZZA CALZONE VARIATION

Make the flatbread recipe as stated on previous page, but divide the rested dough into only 6 portions instead of 12. Make larger disks, and on side of each one, slightly overlap 6 slices of pepperoni. Sprinkle with a pinch of Italian seasoning, then 1-1/2 Tb. shredded mozzarella cheese. Use a dough blade or a wide knife to release one side of the dough from the rolling surface, and gently fold it up and over the filling, pinching it shut on all sides with your fingers. If it tears, the dough is pliable enough to simply patch with another small piece. Fry these the same way as the flatbread.

6 Calzones - per each: 205 cal, 11 g fat (5 g sat), 10 g carb (3 g fiber), 17 g protein

RECIPE NOTES: Excellent hot or cold! Another easily changed recipe - think runzas! and stuff with ground beef and cabbage - think rubens! and stuff with corned beef, sauerkraut, and SF 1000 Island - think sopapillas! and stuff with taco meat, cheese, and salsa - you can stuff a calzone with <u>anything</u>!

Did you know ...

Categories of Sugar Alternatives

Non-nutritive sweeteners are synthesized chemicals that are calorie-free, such a aspartame, saccharine, acesulfame K and sucralose.

Nutritive sweeteners provide calories. Sucrose, dextrose, fructose, sorbitol, mannitol, xylitol, and hydrogenated starch hydrolysate are all nutritive sweeteners.

Polyols are sugar alcohols, such as sorbitol, xylitol, mannitol, maltitol, and maltose. Sugar alcohols can cause intestinal distress and should be consumed with caution.

Extracts of licorice, chicory, kiwi and stevia rebuadiana are natural sweeteners from plants.

Frosting TLC

Frostings are quite high in carbs and may not be suitable for use except on special occasions, but - we all do have special occasions, so ... go for it, once in a while! I find that using a combination of Splenda and maltitol powder works best, since using all maltitol can result in abdominal discomfort, and using all Splenda can result in astronomically high carb counts.

Because these frostings will always be combined with something, and the number of servings may vary each time, I have provided totals for each entire batch as well as the more standard serving size when the yield is 24. Each recipe makes enough to frost one 13x9, two rounds, or 24 cupcakes.

CLASSIC VANILLA CREAM

1/2 cup softened butter
8 oz. softened cream cheese
2 cups granular Splenda™
2-1/2 cups maltitol powder
2-4 Tb. half and half cream
1 tsp. vanilla extract or 1/2 tsp. almond extract

Cream butter and cream cheese. Gradually beat in Splenda, followed by half the cream, the powdered maltitol, and the vanilla extract. Slowly add remaining cream if needed to reach spreading consistency.

Entire batch: 2,678 cal, 178 g fat (110 g sat), 256 g carb (200 g SA), 19 g protein
@ 24 servings, each: 112 cal, 7.4 g fat (4 g sat), 10 g carb (8 g SA)

CHOCOLATE ALMOND

Toast 1 cup almond flour in a 350 F oven until golden. Set aside. Add 4 Tb. cocoa powder and 1 oz. melted unsweetened baking chocolate to classic Vanilla Cream frosting recipe. After spreading the frosting, sprinkle tops and/or sides of item with the toasted almond flour. EASY and impressive looking!

Entire batch: 3,735 cal, 275 g fat (112 g sat), 304 g carb (28 g fiber, 200 g SA), 60 g protein
@ 24 servings, each: 156 cal, 11.4 g fat (4 g sat), 12 g carb (1 g fiber, 8 g SA), 2 g protein

COCONUT-KISSED

Toast 1 cup coconut in a 350 F oven until golden. Set aside. Use coconut, pineapple, or another complimentary flavoring in place of vanilla extract. Mix toasted coconut with 1/2 cup granular Splenda™. After spreading the frosting, sprinkle tops and/or sides of item with the sweetened, toasted coconut.

Entire batch: 2,960 cal, 201 g fat (130 g sat), 276 g carb (6 g fiber, 200 g SA), 22 g protein

@ 24 servings, each: 123 cal, 8.4 g fat (5 g sat), 11 g carb (8 g SA)

The coconut-kissed and chocolate almond variations both make for a very elegant presentation with almost no time OR skill requirements!

MARSHMALLOW CREAM

1-1/2 cups maltitol powder
1/4 cup SF syrup (vanilla or marshmallow flavor)
2 Tb. maltitol syrup
Pinch salt
2 egg whites
Combine syrups and maltitol powder in saucepan. Bring to a boil, beating constantly, and continue to boil and stir for two full minutes. Remove from heat and set aside.
Whip egg whites and salt to soft peaks. While still beating, add hot syrup slowly, in a small stream. Scrape bowl occasionally and continue to beat until frosting looks to be of proper spreading consistency.

Entire batch: 877 cal, 0 g fat, 211 g carb (210 g SA), 7 g protein

@ 24 servings, each: 37 cal, 0 g fat, 8 g carb (8 g SA)

RECIPE NOTES: Kids love this stuff!

Magic Microwave Nut Brittle

1 cup granular Splenda™
1/2 cup maltitol syrup
1-2 tsp. water or SF syrup
1 cup peanuts
1 tsp. butter
1 tsp. vanilla extract
1 tsp. baking soda

Butter a small baking sheet and set aside, or better yet line with a silicone mat.

Combine Splenda and maltitol syrup in large microwaveable bowl, adding small amount of additional liquid only as needed so you can mix the sweeteners. Cook on HIGH power for four minutes.

Add 1 cup nuts and stir well with heat-proof spoon or spatula. Cook on high power for another three to five minutes (as ovens vary in power, this can only be an estimate) until the color changes slightly, to a light golden brown. Remove from microwave and stir in butter and vanilla. Cook for an additional one to two minutes (nuts should be lightly browned), then add baking soda and stir gently until light and foamy. Spread immediately in prepared pan; allow to cool; break into chunks.

12 servings - per each: 55 cal, 3 g fat (0 sat), 6 g carb (4 g SA), 1 g protein

VARIATIONS: Numerous! Excellent with 1/2 cup grated coconut added. Try making walnut brittle with maple extract. How about pecan brittle with cinnamon and nutmeg?

Pecan Delight

This elegant dessert goes together easily in just a few minutes, with a minimum of dirty dishes.

8 oz. cream cheese, softened
3/4 cup granular Splenda™, divided
2 tsp. vanilla extract, divided
3 eggs
1-1/2 cups coarsely chopped pecans
1/4 cup SF maple syrup (You will need to use one that contains sugar alcohols such as maltitol for this dessert to set up properly. Log Cabin™ brand works well.)

Preheat oven to 300 degrees F. Butter or oil 6 small ramekins (if you don't have ramekins, you can substitute small teacups or bowls). Put 4 - 6 cups of water on the heat to come to a boil. In a large glass measuring cup or something else with a pour spout, blend softened cream cheese with 1/2 cup Splenda™, 1 teaspoon vanilla extract, and 1 egg until smooth. Divide the resulting batter equally among the prepared ramekins. Sprinkle chopped nuts over the first layer in equal amounts.

Beat the remaining two eggs, maple syrup, 1 tsp. vanilla extract, and 1/4 cup Splenda™ together. Divide in equal amounts over the contents of the ramekins. Do not mix.

Place the filled ramekins in a baking pan with high sides and place this in the oven before pouring the boiling water into the pan around the ramekins until it comes at least halfway up the sides. Bake for 35 minutes, until lightly golden on top. Remove from water bath, cool for a few moments, run a sharp knife around the edge to release, invert over a serving plate, and serve! You could also cool and serve these desserts directly from the ramekins themselves.

6 servings - per each: 369 cal, 34 g fat (10 g sat), 11 g carb (2 g fiber, 2 g SA), 7 g protein

BERRY DELIGHT: Substitute fresh blueberries for pecans. *Each: 210 cal, 16 g fat (8 g sat), 11 g carb (2 g SA), 7 g protein*

3CPO MUFFINS

2 oz. unsweetened, dried peaches (4 average slices)
1 cup sugar free pineapple flavored syrup
2 cups pecans, coarsely chopped
1-3/4 cups unsweetened coconut
1 cup granular Splenda™,
1-1/2 tsp. ground cinnamon
3 large eggs
4 Tb. oil
1 Tb. molasses
1/2 cup mayonnaise
1 cup protein isolate (soy or wheat)
2 cups almond flour
1/4 tsp. salt
1-1/2 tsp. baking powder (1 tsp. @ altitude)
1 cup cream
2 Tb. butter

At least one hour in advance, bring the syrup to a boil, then slowly drizzle it over the dried peaches, to cover. Set aside and allow peaches to re-hydrate and soften. Toast mixed pecans and coconut in a 350F oven until golden, about 15 minutes; remove from oven and cool. Add cinnamon and Splenda; toss well; set mixture aside.

Puree peach and syrup mixture in a food processor or blender. Transfer to mixing bowl; add eggs, oil, molasses, mayonnaise, and 1-1/2 cups of the reserved cinnamon nut mix. Whisk briskly to blend. Add isolate, nut meal, salt and baking powder to bowl. Slowly pour cream over all. Using a wide rubber spatula, fold ingredients together gently until combined. DO NOT OVER MIX. Scoop out into 24 lined or well greased muffin tins. Divide remaining cinnamon nut mix over top of batter. Bake 15-20 minutes at 350 F, until a toothpick inserted in the center comes out clean. *24 muffins - per each: 274 cal, 24 g fat (4 sat), 8 g carb (2 g fiber), 8 g protein*

VARIATION: Substitute 1 cup dried, diced apricots for the dried peaches. *Add 1 carb per serving.*

ANY FLAVOR MUFFINS

3/4 cup unsweetened, canned coconut milk
1 cup SF Davinci syrup, any flavor desired
1 cup melted butter
1-2 tsp. additional flavoring extracts, if desired (try banana syrup with both coconut or pineapple extracts, orange syrup with cranberries and no extracts, vanilla syrup with blueberries, etc.)
4 large eggs
1 tsp. baking soda (reduce to 3/4 tsp. @ altitude)
1/2 tsp. baking powder
1 cup protein isolate (soy, whey, or wheat)
1/2 cup whole grain wheat or oat flour
1 cup unsweetened shredded coconut
3 Tb. vital wheat gluten

These are just too easy to be this good and this low in carbs! Whisk them up in a single bowl, adding the items in the order listed, then simply divide between 12 greased or lined muffin cups (filling them fairly full). Bake at 350 F for about 20 minutes, until a deep golden. You may see butter bubbling up around the tops as you remove them from the oven; this is to be expected.

12 "plain" muffins - per each: 253 cal, 21 g fat (13 g sat), 5 g carb (1 g fiber), 10 g protein

With these additions, each muffin:

1 cup cranberries - *263 cal, 21 g fat (13 g sat), 8 g carb (1 g fiber), 10 g protein*

1 cup blueberries - *286 cal, 21 g fat (13 g sat), 13 g carb (3 g fiber), 11 g protein*

1/2 cup dried diced apricots - *267 cal, 21 g fat (13 g sat), 9 g carb (1 g fiber), 10 g protein*

2/3 cup cocoa powder and 3/4 cups walnuts - *302 cal, 25 g fat (13 g sat), 9 g carb (2 g fiber), 13 g protein*

BRAN MUFFINS

2 large eggs
3/4 cup oil
3/4 cup half and half cream
1/2 cup granular Splenda™
1 tsp. vanilla (or maple) extract
1 tsp. baking soda (reduce to 3/4 tsp. @ altitude)
3/4 cup plain wheat bran
1/2 cup protein powder
1/4 cup vital wheat gluten
1 cup All Bran Extra Fiber™ cereal
1/2 cup chopped pecans

Preheat oven to 350 F. Line or grease 12 muffin tins very well. Add ingredients to mixing bowl in order listed, scraping sides as needed. Bake 14 to 16 minutes or until they test done.

12 muffins - per each: 246 cal, 20 g fat (3 g sat), 9 g carb (4 g fiber), 7 g protein

BREAD IN A JAR

Baking bread in a jar is a delightful way to present any kind of quick bread for gift giving. This method requires no actual canning, but it will extend the shelf life of the bread for weeks. This is particularly handy when you wish to send a baked good by mail, and it also allows any recipient to not feel obligated to eat your offering right away, at a time when their house may already be overflowing with goodies. You can dress the jars up with a circle of cloth around the lid and some batting or cotton balls for padding, gathered with an elastic band, but I prefer to keep it simple and just affix a colorful, custom label to each jar. If you can get your kids to color some labels, all the better! The label can be as simple as scratch paper you've written on and attached with tape, or you can buy full sized sheets of adhesive-backed stickers to customize and use with an ink-jet printer. To bake any quick bread in a jar, use clean pint size wide-mouth "tapered" jars. Tapered jars are slightly wider at the mouth than at the bottom, and they will allow the bread to slide out easily for serving. They will be labeled as suitable "for Canning or Freezing". You will need a sealing flat and ring closure for each jar. Oil the jars well by drizzling a little oil in the bottom of each jar, and then spread it around evenly using a brush or towel. Fill jars with care, and use a wet, clean paper towel to remove any batter that may drip onto the rims or tops of the jars while you are filling them. You will need to adjust the cooking times and fill levels for each individual recipe, since results will vary depending on the density of each batter. (It can be helpful to bake off one test jar first, when trying a new recipe.) Immediately after removing the jars from the oven, put the sealing flats in place on the top and hand-tighten the ring closure snugly (do not over-tighten). The steam that builds up inside the closed jar will vacuum seal the jar for you as it cools. For longest shelf life, refrigerate after cooling. I have had LC quick breads in my fridge with no loss of quality for up to a month!

CRANBERRY COCONUT BREAD

2 eggs
1 cup unsweetened, canned coconut milk
1/4 cup oil
1/2 cup heavy cream
1/2 cup water
2 tsp. orange extract
1-1/2 cups granular Splenda™
1/2 tsp. salt
1-1/2 Tb. baking powder (scant 4 tsp. @ high altitude)
1 cup vanilla flavor protein powder
1/2 cup vital wheat gluten
3/4 cup almond flour
2 cups unsweetened dried coconut
2 cups whole cranberries, fresh or frozen, chopped

Preheat oven to 350°F. Prepare desired baking pans as needed. In a large bowl, beat 2 eggs. Add coconut milk, oil, cream, water, extract, and Splenda and blend well. Add salt, baking powder, protein powder, and nut flour; blend again. Fold in cranberries and coconut, divide between pans and bake: approximately 35-40 minutes for standard loaves, 20-25 minutes for jars, and 12-14 minutes for muffins. *Makes 30: two loaves @ 15 slices each, five pt. jars* with *6 slices each, or 30 muffins: 125 cal, 9 g fat (3 g sat), 5 g carb (1 g fiber), 5 g protein, each.*

VARIATION: May use 1 cup dried, unsweetened cranberries in place of 2 cups fresh or frozen (same carb count.) Bring 1 cup SF syrup (I like orange flavor) to a boil, add dried, chopped cranberries, and set aside to soften for at least 30 minutes. Fold in the softened berries at the same time as the coconut, otherwise preparing as described.

PUMPKIN SPICE BREAD
1/2 cup sour cream (buttermilk also good)
1/2 cup oil
2 cups granular Splenda™
3 eggs
1 cup SF syrup (vanilla, spice, or another flavor. A maple flavored syrup is also very good here.)
16 oz. can plain pumpkin
4 cups TLC Bake mix
Preheat oven to 350. Whisk ingredients together in the order listed. Grease two loaf pans very well and dust with 1 Tb. of the bake mix. Divide batter among pans and bake for 40-50 minutes, until it tests done. *36 servings - per each: 92 cal, 6 g fat (1 g sat), 6 g carb (1 g fiber), 6 g protein*

ZUCCHINI BREAD
1 cup oil
1/2 cup SF syrup (vanilla, spice, or another flavor)
1 cup granular Splenda™
4 eggs
3 cups TLC Bake mix
4 tsp. ground cinnamon
1 tsp. nutmeg (reduce or omit spices if using spice flavored syrup)
1 pound fresh zucchini, grated (do not peel - you should have about 2 cups, lightly packed)
Preheat oven to 350. Whisk ingredients together in the order listed. Grease two standard loaf pans very well and dust with 1 Tb. of the bake mix. Pour batter into pans and bake about 30 minutes, until it tests done. *24 servings, each: 149 cal, 11 g fat (1 g sat), 6 g carb (1 g fiber), 6 g protein*

Upside-Down Cakes

CRAN-APPLE
6 Tb. softened butter
1 cup chopped almonds or walnuts
1 cup dried unsweetened cranberries, divided
3 small zucchini, about 24 oz. total - 2 unpeeled & thinly sliced, 1 peeled and grated
1 Tb. apple flavor extract
1-1/2 cups granular Splenda™
1 Tb. cinnamon
2 cups TLC bake mix
1/3 cup oil
2 eggs
2/3 cup sour cream

Preheat oven to 350 F. Spread softened butter evenly over bottom of a 13x9 pan. Sprinkle chopped nuts and 1/2 cup of the berries evenly over butter. Toss Splenda with cinnamon, and sprinkle half of this mixture over contents of pan. Press everything down firmly into the butter with the back of a spoon or spatula.

Toss the sliced zucchini in a bowl with the apple extract and 1/4 cup of the remaining Splenda and cinnamon mixture, then layer this mixture over the cranberry-nut- base. Combine bake mix with remaining cinnamon mixture, grated zucchini, oil, eggs, remaining cranberries, and sour cream; pour carefully over layers in pan.

Bake in preheated 350 degree oven for 40 to 45 minutes. Cool in pan for ten minutes, then invert over serving platter to unmold.

24 servings - per each: 147 cal, 11 g fat (3 g sat), 7 g carb (2 g fiber), 5 g protein

VARIATION: Substitute six real apples instead of the 3 zucchini squash. Omit apple extract.

24 servings - per each: 163 cal, 11 g fat (3 g sat), 12 g carb (2 g fiber), 5 g protein

PINEAPPLE
4 Tb. softened butter
8 oz. can pineapple tidbits, in its own juice
1 cup granular Splenda™, divided
1/3 cup SF maple syrup (sorbitol/maltitol based)
1 Tb. molasses
1 egg
1/2 cup sour cream
1 cup melted butter
2 cups TLC Bake mix

Preheat oven to 350. Spread softened butter in the bottom of a large round pan. Sprinkle 1/3 cup of the Splenda over that, followed by the maple syrup substitute.

Press all the juice out of the pineapple tidbits (reserving the juice). Scatter the drained pineapple evenly over butter and sweeteners. Beat the sour cream with the egg and molasses, followed by the melted butter, remaining Splenda, and reserved pineapple juice. Fold in bake mix. Carefully spread batter over layers already in pan. Bake for about 30 minutes, until cake pulls away from sides of pan and tests done. Cool in pan for about ten minutes, then run a knife around the edge to loosen, and invert over serving plate.

@ 12 small servings, each: 287 cal, 23 g fat (13 g sat), 12 g carb (2 g fiber, 1 g SA), 8 g protein

@ 8 "real" servings, each: 431 cal, 35 g fat (19 g sat), 18 g carb (3 g fiber, 1 g SA), 12 g protein

Excellent hot or cold, served with whipped cream or without.

Yeast Bread TLC

When I went low carb and it worked for me, I gave up bread for what I thought was "for good". Especially after tasting a few of the overpriced low carb loaves that some manufacturers still have the nerve to call bread ... yuck! As with other types of food, if I can't "fake" it very *well*, then I prefer to just do without. The bread recipe in Volume I is a good one, and it is pretty darn low in carbs, but the recipes I am about to present are definitely better. They are also correspondingly higher in carbs, however, making them more suitable for people on lifetime maintenance than for people who are still trying to actively lose weight or control specific health conditions through a low carb diet.

Please use caution with the rest of this book if you are new to low carbing. Do not misunderstand the presence of the following recipes, or fool yourself into thinking that I wish to encourage anyone to eat bread. Individual dieters need to determine for themselves whether bread (or "sweets" for that matter) happen to be a "trigger" or a problem for them, and then use or not use those recipes accordingly. I have found that even though I myself used to overeat bread as a food group, I have no urge to do so today. I credit some of that with the fact that I eliminated bread from my diet completely for so long. The recipes that follow have allowed me to enjoy the occasional sandwich, slice of toast and even bagel in the morning again. I hope you can enjoy that, too. Best of all, these recipes have enabled me to feel good about making homemade breads for my non-low carbing friends and family members again. Because ... *let's say it together this time...* "Everyone could use a little TLC!"

Instructions for All TLC Bread Recipes

I used to make fun of people who used bread machines, "back in the day" before I low carbed. Now, I wouldn't be without one. It is really tough to develop the gluten adequately in low carb breads when kneading by hand. A good mixer can do it, but unless you are an old pro at that method already, I think a bread machine does so better and more quickly. The main problem with bread machines and low carb recipes, is that you can never count on a low carb recipe to rise appropriately in the machine manufacturer's standard time cycle. Of course, it just might! But then, it might not. And that will not mean that the recipe is flawed, it will just mean that you need to use the dough cycle only, then form and bake the bread manually. But, guess what - it just so happens that is the best way to do it, anyway! No holes in your loaf from removing the bread paddle afterwards, and you can form regular size loaves if you want, as well as rolls or buns. (If you wish to try baking these recipes off in your machine anyway, I suggest trying a 'rapid' setting first.)

I use a deli slicer to slice all of my homemade bread. Low carb breads are dense enough to slice very thinly, and I typically get a larger yield than is stated here, but I wanted to be realistic about the number of servings most people will get from one loaf when I listed the recipe analysis. If you have trouble slicing your bread thin enough to keep the carb count manageable, consider investing in a good slicer, or try using an electric knife, either of which can and will be used for so much more than bread.

First, gather all your ingredients. I like to mix up many batches of the dry ingredients all at one time, assembly-line style. Extra batches can be vacuum sealed and stored at room temperature, or just tightly sealed and stored in the refrigerator or freezer to be kept on hand for convenience. If you only have to measure out the "wet" ingredients each time you want to make a loaf of bread, the whole process is much quicker.

WHEN USING A MACHINE: Lightly mix the flours, brans, and gluten (dry ingredients) together. Add the salt and sweetener and any eggs, oil, etc. to the other liquid ingredients, and blend well. Add the liquid ingredients, wet ingredients, and yeast to the machine separately in the order recommended by the manufacturer. Typically, this means pouring the liquids in, followed by the dry ingredients, with the yeast going in on the top in a small well, last. Process on 'dough' cycle.

A good tweak for all bread recipes: Use a little less water than the recipe calls for the first time around, since you can always add more, but getting it back is impossible.

WHEN USING A MIXER OR YOUR HANDS:
In a small bowl, combine the yeast and any sweeteners in warm recipe liquids. Make sure the liquid you use is only baby-bottle warm - adding yeast to water that is too hot can kill yeast, which is a living organism and does have a shelf life. Let the yeast mixture stand until gets foamy, about 10 minutes. If the reconstituted yeast does not begin to foam and "grow" by the end of the ten minutes, it may not be any good - check the expiration date, and then try again with a new batch of yeast.

Combine all dry ingredients, and stir or whisk to blend them well. In a large mixing bowl, combine the yeast mixture with any remaining cream, the oil, eggs, and 1-1/2 cups of the dry ingredients; beat well. Continue to add the dry ingredients, 1/2 cup at a time, stirring well after each addition and reserving the last quarter to half cup of dry ingredients for "flouring" the kneading surface. Turn the formed dough out onto a "floured" surface, and begin kneading. Knead until smooth and elastic, perhaps 10 minutes - more or less kneading may be needed, depending on an individual's technique. This is the part that is hard to teach, the "feel" for properly kneaded dough, which comes only from experience, and which is difficult to attain with low carb ingredients.

Lightly oil or butter the mixing bowl you used previously, place the dough back in the bowl, then turn it over once, so as to coat the entire surface lightly

FABULOUS FAKES

with oil. While kneading, bring 2 cups of water to a full boil inside your microwave oven. Cover the bowl containing the dough with a clean, slightly damp cloth, or some plastic wrap, and place the whole thing inside the microwave. (Just push the warm water into one corner and leave it there, to continue warming the area slightly while the dough rises.) Leave the dough to rise inside the closed, turned off microwave until doubled in volume, roughly 40-60 minutes. (You don't NEED the warm water near the dough while it rises; neither do you NEED to let dough rise in a microwave - any warm, draft-free place will work - this is just the way I always do it.)

ALL METHODS:
Grease a standard size bread pan well. Poke deeply down into the risen dough with two fingers, to deflate it, then knead it lightly two or three times to remove any remaining air. Roll the dough out into a long rectangle slightly longer than the bread pan, on a nonstick or lightly floured surface. Starting at the long side of the rectangle, roll the dough up tightly. Don't be gentle - go ahead and pinch the seam firmly after every turn, along its entire length. Push one finger into each end of the roll, to shorten it to an appropriate length, then tuck it into the greased pan, seam side down. Cover with a slightly damp cloth and let it rise in a warm place until doubled in size, usually 30-40 minutes. Preheat oven to 350 F. Bake for 50-60 minutes, or until the loaf has good color and sounds hollow when tapped with a knuckle. Cool thoroughly on a wire rack before wrapping and storing (to prevent possible condensation resulting in soggy bread.) I usually cover cooling bread with a clean cloth and leave it out for several hours or even overnight before slicing, then wrapping tightly to store in the refrigerator for up to one week. Freeze if longer storage is required.

TO MAKE BUNS INSTEAD OF BREAD:
Any of the bread recipes can be made into 16 buns instead of a loaf of bread. Use a sharp knife to divide the dough into equal sized portions, then start tuck-

ing and pulling the edges of the dough under and up into the center of the bottom of the ball, smoothing the top as you go. Place balls of dough, smooth sides up, at least one inch apart on a greased baking sheet; cover, brush tops with heavy cream, and allow to rise until doubled in size. For hamburger buns, simply flatten the balls into a large disk before allowing to rise. For hot dogs, form into longer, skinnier rolls. Shorten total baking time for rolls to 20-30 minutes.

You can form other shapes of rolls with any of my recipes, as desired, including deep-dish pizza crusts - but I can't consider a pizza crust made with these recipes to be "truly low" in carbs, considering the much smaller yield, so I won't present it that way.

All-Purpose Light Oat Bread

1/2 cup melted butter
1 cup plain yogurt
1/2 cup half and half cream
2 eggs
1/4 cup granular Splenda™

1-1/2 cups oat flour
1 cup barley flour (or whole wheat pastry flour)
1 cup vital wheat gluten
1/2 cup flax meal (use golden for lightest appearance)

2 tsp. active dry yeast - reduce to 1.5 tsp. at high altitude.

@ 24 slices - per slice: 127 cal, 6 g fat (2 g sat), 10 g carbohydrate (1 g fiber), 6 g protein
@ 16 buns - per bun: 190 cal, 9 g fat (4 g sat), 16 g carb (2 g fiber), 9 g protein

VARIATION: Use oat bran in place of flax meal. Adds 1 carb per slice or bun.

Cheesy Garlic Pinwheels / Bread

After punching down risen light oat dough and rolling it out into the rectangle shape, spread dough evenly with 3 Tb. softened butter, 2 Tb. grated onion, and 2 tsp. minced garlic. Sprinkle with 1/3 cup shredded cheddar and 2 Tb. grated Parmesan cheese. Roll up tightly from the long side, pinching seams shut, as described in general bread instructions. For rolls, use a sharp knife to slice the roll of dough crosswise into 16 even portions, which are risen and baked cut sides down, sides touching.

@ 24 slices - per slice: 149 cal, 8 g fat (4 g sat), 11 g carbohydrate (1 g fiber), 7 g protein

@ 16 buns - per bun: 224 cal, 13 g fat (6 g sat), 16 g carb (2 g fiber), 10 g protein

Cinnamon Rolls / Swirl Bread

After punching down risen light oat dough and rolling it out into a rectangle shape about 16 inches long, spread dough evenly with 2 Tb. softened butter and sprinkle that with a mixture of 1 Tb. cinnamon and 1/3 cup granular Splenda™. Roll up tightly from the long side, pinching seams shut, as described in general bread instructions. For rolls, use a sharp knife to slice the roll of dough crosswise into 16 even portions, which are risen and baked, cut sides down, with sides touching.

@ 24 slices - per slice: 137 cal, 7 g fat (3 g sat), 11 g carbohydrate (1 g fiber), 6 g protein

@ 16 buns - per bun: 206 cal, 11 g fat (5 g sat), 17 g carb (2 g fiber), 9 g protein

Fruit & Nut Loaf

1 cup dried unsweetened cranberries
1 cup cinnamon or orange flavored SF syrup (could use other flavors or even other fruits, as desired)
1/2 cup melted butter
1/2 cup heavy cream
1/2 cup water
2 eggs
1/2 tsp. salt
2-3 tsp. cinnamon (or orange zest with cinnamon syrup, etc.)
1/2 tsp. freshly grated nutmeg
1/4 tsp. ground cloves
1/4 tsp. ground ginger
1/2 cup granular Splenda™
1/2 cup wheat bran
1/2 cup oat bran
1/2 cup whole wheat flour
1 cup oat flour
1 cup vital wheat gluten
1 cup unsweetened coconut
1/2 cup chopped pecans
2-1/4 tsp. (1 pkg.) active dry yeast - reduce by 1/2 tsp. @ high altitude

Heat syrup to boiling; add dried fruit and set aside for 30-60 minutes, to cool and soften. Most of the liquid should be absorbed before proceeding. Melt butter. Add water, cream, eggs, salt, spices, and sweetener; beat lightly; add softened berries and set aside. In a separate container, lightly mix the flours, gluten, bran, coconut, and nuts. Add wet and dry ingredients to bread machine along with yeast, in order suggested by manufacturer. May also be mixed by hand. Batter may be slightly sticky. Allow to rise once, punch down, form into a loaf, allow to rise again, then bake at 350 F until loaf sounds hollow when tapped and is a uniform golden brown in color, 45-55 minutes. *Makes 24 slices - per slice: 113 cal, 5 g fat (2 g sat), 10 g carb (2 g fiber), 5 g protein*

VARIATION: May use 1/2 cup dried diced apricots in place of 1 cup cranberries.

Rustic Pumpernickel Rye

4 Tb. oil
1-1/2 cups warm water
1 egg
1 Tb. molasses
1 tsp. salt
1 Tb. onion powder
2 tsp. cocoa powder
1 tsp. instant coffee granules
Beat the above ingredients lightly and set aside.

In a separate container, blend together:
2 cups pumpernickel meal or dark rye flour
1/2 cup wheat bran
1/2 cup whole wheat pastry flour
1 cup vital wheat gluten

Add wet and dry ingredients to a bread machine along with 1 pkg. yeast (reduce by 1/2 tsp @ alt) in order recommended by bread machine manufacturer and process on 'Dough' (or follow alternate TLC by-hand assembly instructions on page 124, dissolving yeast first in warm water and molasses.)

Punch down risen dough, knead several turns to in-sure that no air bubbles remain, and form it into one large round loaf shape. Allow to rise again on well greased or lined baking sheet, covered, until doubled in size (about 40 minutes), then bake at 350 for about 40 minutes.

24 slices - per slice: 88 cal, 3 g fat (0 g sat), 10 g carb (1 g fiber) 5 g protein

RECIPE NOTES: Bake in a standard loaf shape, if desired. I created my Garlic Schmear specially to go with this warm bread. I make the duo for every party I host these days, and my guests delight in ripping apart the warm, round loaf themselves. This is my hands-down, all-time, favorite bread recipe, and it is the ONLY one I have never "tinkered" with in any way since the day I created it.

Yogi Bread

My family's favorite low carb bread so far - named in honor of our 2003 Yellowstone vacation, in preparation for which I originally created this flax-free variation of the All Purpose Light bread recipe.

1/2 cup melted butter
1-1/2 cups warm water
2 eggs
1/2 tsp. salt
1/4 cup granular Splenda™

3 Tb. dry milk powder (or plain whey protein)
1-3/4 cups oat flour
1 cup whole wheat flour
1/2 cup oat bran
1 cup gluten
1 pkg. yeast (2-1/4 tsp - reduce to 1-3/4 tsp. at high altitude)

@ 24 slices - per slice: 118 cal, 6 g fat (2 g sat), 11 g carb (1 g fiber), 6 g protein

@ 16 buns - per bun: 177 cal, 9 g fat (4 g sat), 17 g carb (2 g fiber), 9 g protein